GREAT Shipwrecks
of the 20th CENTURY

THOMAS E. BONSALL

GALLERY BOOKS
An Imprint of W. H. Smith Publishers Inc.
112 Madison Avenue
New York City 10016

© Copyright 1988 in U.S.A. by Bookman Dan!, Inc.
Published in the United States of America by Bookman Publishing,
an Imprint of Bookman Dan Inc.
P. O. Box 13492, Baltimore, MD 21203

Exclusive Distribution by Gallery Books,
an Imprint of W. H. Smith Publishers Inc.
112 Madison Avenue, New York City, NY 10016

ISBN 0-8317-7781-8

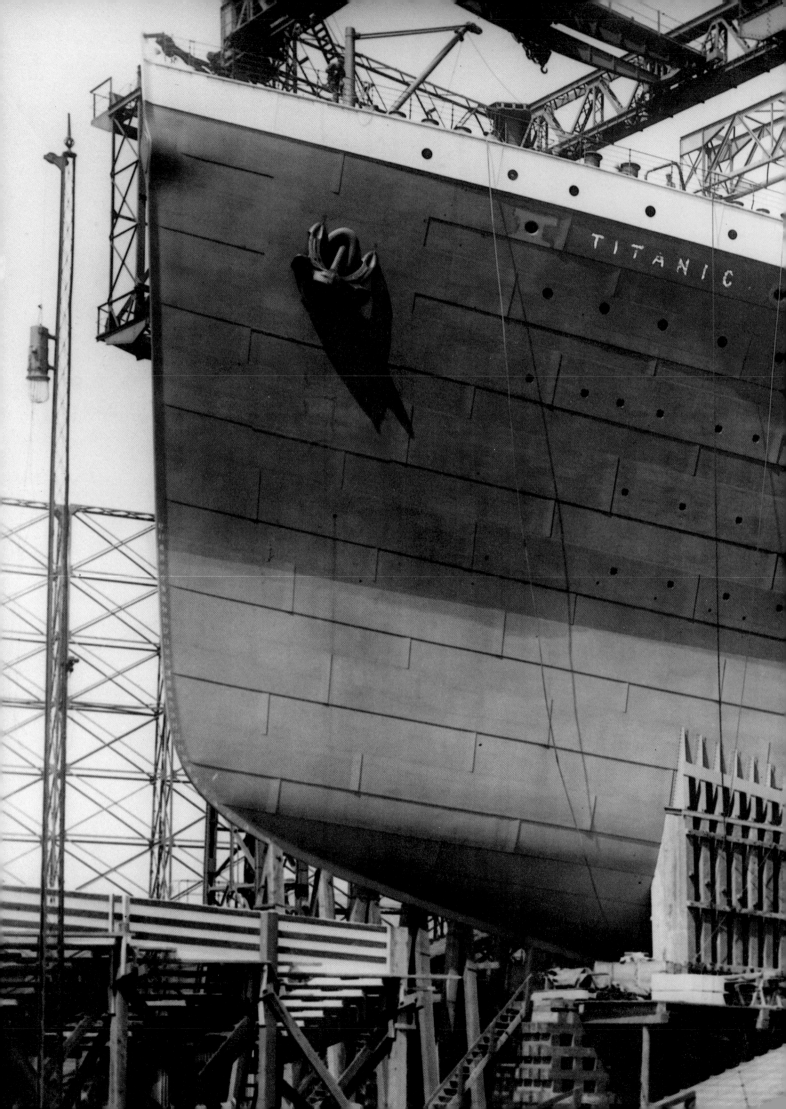

PREFACE

Why are certain shipwrecks such a source of public fascination? Hundreds of people died in coal mine accidents in the United States in 1956, yet, while most of those tragic incidents garnered little or no national publicity, the country's attention was riveted to the fate of the *Andrea Doria*, a disaster that cost the lives of only 51. Or, to bring it to a more modern perspective, tens of thousands died in motor vehicle accidents in this country in 1986. Most of these accidents were barely reported, yet the discovery of an ancient wreck responsible for the demise of a mere 1,500 souls was front page news for days: I refer, of course, to the *Titanic*.

The *Titanic* is, indeed, the granddaddy of all shipwrecks. It has been elevated by this point to the status of myth or legend and probably will remain a part of our culture for centuries to come. Last year, I published a book on the *Titanic* and her two sisters (the *Olympic* and the *Britannic*) that sold over 40,000 copies in hardcover during the first three weeks it was on sale.† Even my distributor was amazed at the success of that book. Why has the *Titanic* become a focus of such popular attraction?

As I explained then, I believe it has to do with the fact that the *Titanic* was more than just a ship to people. It came to symbolize an era in which material progress had assumed an almost religious status.

People in Europe and the New World alike had come to believe in the perfectability of man. Man could, if the proper disciplines were followed, rise above anything. Even nature. Even his own inherent imperfection. (This belief was not limited to capitalist cultures, either. Witness the efforts of the Soviets to create the New Socialist Man in countries they controlled.) The *Titanic* was the crown jewel in this philosophy. Its tragic sinking was a trauma from which western culture has arguably never recovered. It changed for all time the way in which we regard ourselves and our place in the world around us. That is why the *Titanic* has reached the level of mythology in our culture, a position it is not likely to soon relinquish.

Indeed, the *Titanic* legend has reached such a status in the popular culture that nearly all other steamship wrecks have faded into near total obscurity. It is almost as if the *Titanic* is the only ship that ever sank. That is ridiculous, of course; there have been any number of terrible sea disasters. It was the nature of the ship itself combined with the magnitude of the loss of life that created the legend.

The same process is at work on a smaller scale with other shipwrecks. So, what about those other important shipwrecks? The *Titanic* was not, after all, the worst loss of life in maritime history. Nor was the *Titanic* the largest liner ever sunk. The French liner, *Normandie* (82,799 tons), and the *Seawise University* (83,673 tons, formerly the Cunard Line's *Queen Elizabeth*) were substantially larger. The *Titanic's* own virtually unknown sister, the *Britannic*, was slightly larger, as well. None of these ships were in service as passenger liners at the time they sank, however.

The probable worst loss of life on a liner was recorded on January 30, 1945, when the 25,000 ton refugee ship, *Wilhelm Gustloff*, was sunk off Danzig in

†*Titanic, The Story of the Great White Star Line Trio: The Olympic, the Titanic and the Britannic*, which was also distributed by Gallery Books, and is currently in print. I would modestly recommend it to anyone interested in some of the lesser-known aspects of the *Titanic* story.

the closing days of World War II. According to reports at the time, 7,700 persons may have died. In fact, the estimates bottom out at around 6,000 and run as high as 9,000. Futhermore, there were at least two similar tragedies during that war that individually may have accounted for death totals well in excess of 5,000, thus making World War II unquestionably the grisliest period in history for loss of life on board ship.

Many of the steamship calamities that have entered the public consciousness in the West do not even appear on the list of real disasters. Probably the two best-known incidents since the *Lusitania* have been the *Morro Castle* and the *Andrea Doria*.

The *Morro Castle*, a medium-sized American steamer en route from Havana to New York, burned off the coast of New Jersey in September, 1934, most likely as the result of arson. Only 133 people died (scarcely worth mentioning in the league of great shipwrecks) and the ship never actually sank. It washed ashore at Asbury Park and smoldered there for days, making for quite a tourist sensation.

The 29,000 ton *Andrea Doria*, pride of the Italian Line, collided with the Swedish liner *Stockholm* off Nantucket in July, 1956. A total of 51 people died and the sinking of the *Andrea Doria* made the front page of nearly every daily newspaper in North America. Next to the *Titanic* and the *Lusitania*, the *Andrea Doria* is probably the only sinking that has retained any kind of impact on the popular mind.

The *Titanic* remains both the worst loss of life involving an ocean liner in regular service and the largest liner ever sunk in regular service. Indeed, the 45,000 ton *Titanic* remains the only liner over 31,000 tons ever sunk in regular service, so it is the largest by quite a margin. The *L'Atlantique*, at 42,500 tons was nearly as big, but was not in passenger service at the time and did not sink.

The *Lusitania*, second in size among liners that sank in regular service and in loss of life among liners *per se*, drops to third or even fourth in loss of life if one uses a broad description of what constitutes a passenger ship. The Mississippi river boat, *Sultana*, blew up in April, 1865, near Memphis, Tennessee, with a loss of around 1,450 people.

The rankings for loss of life among scheduled passenger ships are as follows (again, using a broad definition of what constitutes a scheduled passenger ship):

1. 1,503 lost, *Titanic*, April 15, 1912, in the North Atlantic.

2. 1,450 lost, *Sultana*, April 27, 1865, in the Mississippi River near Memphis.

3. 1,198 lost, *Lusitania*, May 7, 1915, off the Irish coast.

4. 1,172 lost, *Toya Maru*, September 26, 1954, in the Tsugaru Strait off Japan.

5. 1,031 lost, *General Slocum*, June 15, 1904, in the Hudson River.

6. 1,012 lost, *Empress of Ireland*, May 29, 1914, in the St. Lawrence River.

7. 1,000 lost, *Kichemaru*, September 28, 1912, off the Japanese coast.

8. 1,000 lost, *Hsin Yu*, August 29, 1916, off the Chinese coast.

9. 1,000 lost, *Hong Kong*, March 18, 1921, in the South China Sea.

10. 812 lost, *Eastland*, July 24, 1915, in the Chicago River.

A couple of things are striking about this list. First, the second decade of this century was clearly the worst time to go for a cruise. Six of the ten worst losses of life occurred between 1912 and 1916, and, of these, only one--the *Lusitania*--was war-related. Second, it is astonishing how many of these tragedies occurred, literally, within sight of land. The *Lusitania* was only six miles off the Irish coast when it sank. The *Sultana*, the *General Slocum*, the *Empress of Ireland*, and the *Eastland* were all sunk in rivers. In what has to be the most bizarre case of all, the *Eastland* was still at the pier in Chicago when it capsized--it hadn't even set sail!

How, one is prompted to ask, do hundreds of souls die a few yards from land? Or, in the case of the *Eastland*, while sitting at the pier? The answer is: bad luck, mostly. The *Sultana*, as has been noted, blew up. That was an ever-present hazard with riverboats in the 19th century and the *Sultana* was unique only in the number of people aboard when disaster struck. The *General Slocum* burned, too, and, as the subsequent investigation revealed, was woefully lacking in usable safety gear (there were a lot of life preservers that wouldn't float, and deficiencies of that nature).

The *Empress of Ireland* was involved in a collision that took place at night in a dense fog. The ship capsized and sank in 14 minutes and those below decks--which included most of the unfortunate passengers--hardly had a chance.

A similar thing happened to the *Eastland*. It was boarding passengers for a Sunday excursion when it suddenly rolled over into the Chicago River. It was disclosed later that the ship was known to be top heavy and was notoriously "tender" in heavy weather. On that fateful Sunday, it had been grossly overloaded and, what was worse, most of the passengers clambered toward the open spaces on the upper decks until the ship's center of gravity fatally shifted. Those on the wrong side of the ship and those still below decks were gone in a matter of seconds.

In at least some of these worst cases, one has to take the precise death counts with a grain of salt. Even with the *Titanic*, which had formal passenger and crew manifests, there is still debate over exactly how many died. Some of the other totals--the 1,400 on the *Sultana* and those on the sinkings in the Orient--have to be estimates. It is doubtful that any of them had any sort of formal passenger lists, for instance. Investigators at the time probably just counted the corpses and made an educated guess as to how many others were never found. The three cataclysmic sinkings in World War II previously mentioned warrant the same caveat. It is certain that there was numbing loss of life, although the figures given are clearly approximations and are still hotly debated in certain cases.

When the list of sinkings in recent decades is examined, a depressing number of them are found to occur in the Third World. Even into our own day, safety standards seem to be depressingly lax in certain regions of the world and the serious losses of life that happen nowadays are mostly confined to Asian countries.

The fact that these recurring disasters are all but invisible to us in the West is no doubt a function of our cultural myopia. This is what someone once referred to as the "Indian Bus Plunge Syndrome." We all know that people in much of the Third World live in conditions miserable beyond our comprehension. Every now and then, at almost predictable intervals, a bus loaded to the beams with incredible numbers of people (sitting, crouching in the aisles, hanging from the sides, clinging to the roof, etc.) will plunge off a cliff and scores of people will die. The story generally appears on page 27, section "B" of your daily newspaper.

We pay little or no attention to such tragedies because they are so far removed from our western experience. They might as well be happening on a different planet. (Naturally, it is entirely different if a few Americans happen to be on board! Then, it is front page news all across the United States.)

We do still have tragedies in our own part of the world, of course. Shortly before this was written, the English Channel ferry *Herald of Free Enterprise* capsized off the coast of Belgium, taking an estimated 188 people to their deaths in the worst English Channel accident in recent times. This has been yet another disaster that took place within sight of land.

In this book I have attempted to cover the most important scheduled passenger liner wrecks of the 20th Century. I have elected to interpret the term "shipwreck" in the loosest possible way so as to include all means--save financial--by which major ocean liners met untimely fates.

This book by no means exhausts the list of ships that have come to grief, though. Lloyds of London lists between 4,000-5,000 ships alone that have disappeared without a trace during the past 125 years. The number of collisions, wrecks and fires of all kinds is surely in the tens--if not hundreds--of thousands. Since this book is intended primarily for a North American market, I have been governed by a desire to cover those ships that are likely to be of the most intense interest to my probable readers. Moreover, I have tried to apportion the coverage so as to give greater emphasis to those shipwrecks likely to peak that interest. That means ocean liner coverage, primarily.

There are a few exceptions to my ocean-liners-only policy, such as the riverboats *Eastland* and *General Slocum*, which were tragedies of such magnitude that they demanded inclusion. I have not included any military calamities, although I have included important ocean liners that were sunk in wartime, whether on military missions or not.

This book is, therefore, not intended to be a comprehensive listing of all shipwrecks of the 20th Century, or even of all ocean liner shipwrecks of the 20th Century. The reader should, however, find all of the most important ones here. If I have over-looked any favorites, my apologies.

What about the future? Could a *Titanic* disaster--or, even an *Andrea Doria* disaster--happen again? It is increasingly unlikely, if only because there are so few large liners still plying the seas. As the *Andrea Doria* and the *Stockholm* demonstrated, however, even modern safety devices cannot guarantee safe passage. The respective bridge crews of the two ships literally stood there and watched the collision develop on radar and did nothing about it because it was obviously the other ship's problem. Where people are involved, disaster is always possible--if not probable.

•　•　•

Most of the material included on these pages has been drawn from my personal archive of steamship memorabilia, photos, brochures, etc. No one has it all, though--a rude fact brought home to me each time I attempt to do a book--and I am invariably sent surrying to seek assistance from those who have what I need to do the job properly.

The Steamship Historical Society of America was of tremendous help with filling the gaps in this particular volume. Their library, which is located here in Baltimore, Maryland, is a wonderful resource for anyone doing serious research into ocean liners, riverboats or any of a number of steamship topics. Their resident librarian, Laura Brown, was most cooperative throughout my research. Her cheerful attitude and profound knowledge of the material entrusted to her care made my job not only easier, but more rewarding, as well.

I would like to take a little space here to say something about the society:

The Steamship Historical Society of America, Inc., was established in 1935 to bring together amateur and professional historians interested in the history of steam navigation and now has a world-wide membership of more than 3,000.

The Society's quarterly journal, *STEAMBOAT BILL,* has been published continuously since 1940. Each issue contains original articles about steamships and other vessels past and present. Of particular interest are regular reports about the present-day shipping scene, including information regarding the disposition of the growing number of ocean liners wasting away in unwilling retirement.

The Society maintains one of the largest libraries in North America devoted exclusively to steamships and steamship history. The library is located at the University of Baltimore (Maryland). It has a centrally situated downtown location about two short blocks from the Amtrak station. Considering how convenient it is, it is a shame it is not more heavily used by steamship researchers. Anyone in the New York-to-Washington corridor (which includes a sizeable percentage of the U.S. population) could, by using the train, arrive at the library in the morning, do hours of research, and, literally, be home in time for dinner.

The collection includes books, periodicals, special reports, pamphlets, brochures, menus, correspondence, records, drawings, postcards and photographs. The extensive photographic collection alone totals over 60,000 prints--not counting more than 30,000 negatives and more than 25,000 picture postcards.

Copies of any pictures not otherwise restricted may be purchased either by mail or in person and the library is open to anyone wanting to do serious research. It is, of course, always a good idea to contact the library in advance of any visit. Inquiries should be addressed to: Librarian, SSHSA Collection, University of Baltimore Library, 1420 Maryland Avenue, Baltimore, MD 21201.

Chapter One
SHIPWRECKS, 1900-1909

The first decade of the new century saw nearly 50 sea disasters involving passenger ships. The vast majority of these involved liners of less than 5,000 tons built in the 1880s and resulted in no loss of life. In fact, only five disasters resulted in more than 100 lives lost. The worst of these involved a day steamer in the Hudson River off New York City--the *General Slocum*--on which 1,031 perished by fire in one of the worst passenger ship disasters ever.

The major shipping news of the decade was the development of the modern "super" liners, liners displacing more than 15,000 tons. The White Star Line started the trend with its landmark 17,272 ton *Oceanic* of 1899--the first ship to exceed the mid-nineteenth century *Great Eastern* in length. It was widely believed that the new class of liners were too big and too safely designed to sink, a belief that was to be proven tragically wrong with the sinking of the

46,000 ton *Titanic* in 1912.

None-the-less, vast strides in safety at sea had been achieved. Fewer passenger ships were destined to come to grief in future decades and major losses of life would become less frequent.

Be that as it may, sailing the seas remained a fairly risky business in the first decade of the century. Despite improvements in ship construction, ships were still navigated much as they always had been, by wit, keen eyesight and

E. Gabriel. 00.

Mailed from London Fb. 27 S.S. Bavarian (Allan Line

luck. Radar and sonar were still far off dreams, a fact which explains the number of collisions and wrecks that littered the decade and which probably also explains the two liners that simply disappeared without a trace. Fire, that other great seafarer's nightmare, was also improperly understood. Fire safety standards were measurably increased due to the *General Slocum* disaster and also in the wake of the Great Hoboken Fire of 1900, which consumed the North German Lloyd piers on the Hudson River directly across from New York City.

The first passenger ship to be lost in the new century was the *Cuvier*, a 2,229 ton Lamport & Holt liner. Built in 1883, the *Cuvier* collided with the *Douvre* off the East Goodwin lightship on March 9, 1900. The sinking of the *Cuvier* cost the lives of 26 persons. The 4,661 ton *Mexican*, of the Union Steamship Co., and the 2,298 ton *Devenum*, of the Portugese Andresen Line, also came to grief, but fortunately with no loss of life. On June 30th, the Great Hoboken Fire occurred. Several North German Lloyd ships were damaged or destroyed and 99 persons lost their lives on the 4,967 ton *Saale*.

Above top, the Tantallon Castle was one of the first shipwrecks of the century (Steamship Historical Society/ University of Baltimore Library).

Opposite, the Allan Line's Bavarian holds the dubious distinction of being the first ship over 10,000 tons ever sunk.

The second year of the century saw the first major loss of life at sea when the 3,548 ton *City of Rio de Janeiro* was wrecked off San Francisco on February 22, 1901. The *City of Rio de Janeiro* was built in 1878 and operated by the Pacific Mail Steamship Co. between California and the Far East. It left Yokohama, Japan, on February 2nd and reached San Francisco in the early morning hours of February 22nd. Against the advice of the harbor pilot, the captain insisted on attempting to pass through the Golden Gate in the morning fog. The *City of Rio de Janeiro* was wrecked on the rocks and went down with the loss of 105 lives--including the captain.

Other shipwrecks in 1901 included the 5,636 ton *Tantallon Castle* of the Union-Castle Line wrecked off Cape Town, the 3,912 ton *Lusitania* of the Elder Dempster Line wrecked near Cape Race, the 3,396 ton *Armenia* of the Anchor Line wrecked near St. John and the 2,101 ton *Mexico* of the Spanish Trans-Atlantic Co., wrecked off Portugal. None of these wrecks involved loss of life.

The spring of 1902 saw the worst disaster of the decade at sea when the 2,119 ton *Camorta* sank in a cyclone in the Gulf of Martaban while on a voyage from Madras to Rangoon. The *Camorta*, built in 1880, was operated by the British India Steam Navigation Co. All hands were lost, including 650 passengers and 89 crewmen.

The other sinkings in 1902 were less catastrophic. The 4,752 ton *Waesland*, of the American Line, collided with the *Harmonides* on March 5th. Two persons lost their lives in the disaster, which occurred off Anglesey. The 3,613 ton *Grecian* of the Allan Line was wrecked off Halifax on February 9th and the 4,562 ton *Lake Superior*, operated by Elder Dempster, was wrecked near St. John on March 31st, both without loss of life.

The following year was relatively uneventful. The only noteworthy loss was the 2,209 ton *Bretagne*, operated by the Societe Generale des Transports Maritimes (SGTM), wrecked at Bahia on September 12th, fortunately without loss of life.

362. - CHERBOURG. - Le Transatlantique allemand
"*Kaiser Wilhelm der Grosse*", après l'abordage avec l' " *Orinoco*

Collection P. B., Cherbourg

In 1904, the disaster list was unfortunately more lengthy. The worst of these involved the Scandanavian American Line's 3,310 ton *Norge*, wrecked off Rockall on June 28th. Built in 1881, the *Norge* did not join the Scandanavian American Line until 1898. Operated on the Copenhagen to New York run, the *Norge* was

Above opposite, the Kaiser Wilhelm der Grosse, which collided with the steamer Orinoco.
Below opposite, Prinzessin Victoria Luise, sunk off Jamaica.
Above, the Dakota, the largest American steamer of her day, was wrecked near Yokohama.
Below, the ill-fated City of Rio de Janeiro (Steamship Historical Society/ University of Baltimore Library).

run up on the rocks at Rockall and sank with an estimated loss of 550 persons, most of them immigrants bound for America.

Other wrecks in 1904 entailed no loss of life. They included the 5,655 ton *Kurfurst*, of the Hamburg East-Africa Line, wrecked off Portugal on May 6th and the 6,901 ton *Australia*, of the

P & O Line, wrecked near Melbourne on June 29th.

The list of ships come to grief continued to climb in 1905, although without any reported loss of life. On February 7th, the 1,779 ton *Damara*, of Furness, Withy & Co., foundered off Musquodoboit, on February 16th, the 6,077 ton *Orizaba*, of the Orient Line, was wrecked off Fremantle, on June 23rd, the 4,686 ton *Chodoc*, of Chargeur Reunis, was wrecked near Gardafui, in July the 3,869 ton *Rohilla Maru*, of Toyo Kisen Kabushiki Kaisha, was wrecked in the China Inland Sea, on September 5th, the 4,380 ton *Cyril*, of the Booth Line, sank following a collision with the *Anselm* (also of the Booth Line) in Amazon River, and November 5th the 10,376 ton *Bavarian*, of the Allan Line, was wrecked on Wye Rock near Montreal. The *Bavarian* became the first passenger ship exceeding 10,000 tons ever lost.

The next year, 1906, saw the worst disaster of the decade, the burning of the *General Slocum*, as well as the fourth worst disaster, the loss of the *Sirio*. The 4,141 ton *Sirio*, of the Raggio Line (Societa Italiana di Transporti Maritimi Raggio & Co.), was built in 1883 and worked the Genoa-South American run to Montevideo and Buenos Aires. On August 4th, while en route to Cadiz, the *Sirio* was wrecked on the rocks off Hormigas Island. The immigrants on board panicked, and, in the ensuing bedlam, an estimated 442 people died. The remainer of the 772 passengers and crew were rescued by fishing boats. It was later reported that the ship had been engaged in the illegal embarkation of Spanish immigrants, which explained why she was sailing outside the normal shipping lanes.

On November 21, 1906, the North German Lloyd liner, *Kaiser Wilhelm der Grosse*, was rammed by the British steamer, *Orinoco*, off Cherbourg. The *Kaiser* was badly damaged and five passengers were killed.

The year 1907 was calm, indeed, compared with what had gone before. The big loss of life of the year transpired on February 24th when the 4,213 ton *Imperatrix* was wrecked off Crete. Forty souls were lost. The only other significant loss of life took place on the 2,679 ton *Poitou*, of the SGTM, which came to grief on May 7th when it was wrecked off Uruguay taking 20 persons with her. On the other hand, the biggest news that year was the wreck of a ship that involved no loss of life at all. The *Dakota*, the pride of the American merchant marine, and the flagship of the Great Northern Steam Ship Company, was wrecked on the 7th of March through sheer carelessness near Yokohama, Japan, and declared a total loss.

WHITE STAR LINE

The following year, 1908, saw only three authenticated deaths among the ocean liners plying the seas. All of them perished in March aboard the 6,224 ton *Newark Castle*, of the Union-Castle Line, when it was wrecked near Durban. On the other hand, the 2,926 ton *Neustria* of the Fabre Line disappeared between New York and Marseille with an undetermined passenger and crew compliment. On the 27th of October it sailed from New York and no trace of her was ever seen again. While the *Neustria* was able

Opposite, the Republic.
Above, the badly mangled Florida limps into port (Steamship Historical Society/ University of Baltimore Library).

Following pages, for a month in 1910, the 13,000 ton Minnehaha was stranded in the Scilly Isles. It survived only to be lost in WW I.

to accommodate 1,118 passengers, fully 1,100 of them were steerage, i.e., immigrants travelling from the old world to the new. It is unlikely the ship would have had many passengers on the return voyage.

The last year of the decade, 1909, saw several of the most significant--or, at least interesting-- shipwrecks. On January 23rd, the White Star Line's 15,378 ton liner *Republic* collided at 5:30 in the morning 175 miles east of the Ambose Lightship with the Italian immigrant liner, *Florida*. The *Republic* sank the next day, but only four people died due to the first ever use of wireless for a distress call. The *Baltic*, also of the White Star Line, was nearby and rescued nearly all the passengers and crew aboard both ships. The *Florida* eventually limped into port.

On June 10th, the 10,606 ton *Slavonia* was wrecked--with no loss of life--giving her the dubious

distinction of being the first Cunard liner ever lost in peacetime. The following month, the 9,339 ton *Waratah* disappeared without a trace off the coast of South Africa. There is circumstantial evidence that she may have exploded, but she did not carry a wireless and no wreckage of any kind was ever found. She took 92 passengers to their deaths.

In August, 1909, the 12,952 ton *Lucania*, another Cunarder, burned at Liverpool. The *Lucania*, launched in 1893, had been the first Cunarder to give up her sails and rely solely on steam for power. She was deemed too old to repair and was scrapped. Finally, on November 14th, the old Messageries Maritimes liner, the 2,370 ton *La Seyne*, which dated back to 1873, collided with the British liner *Onda* while en route to Singapore. Of her 162 passengers, 101 perished.

Horror on the East River:
The Burning of the General Slocum

There was nothing remarkable about the *General Slocum*. She was but one of many boats making day trips on the waterways in and around New York City. When she pulled away from her East River pier on the morning of June 15, 1904, few could even have imagined the horror that was about to ensue. On board were well over a thousand persons, including hundreds of women and children, on a church outing. In command was Captain W. H. Schaick.

As the *General Slocum* churned its way up the river past 83rd Street at an estimated 10 knots, the first whiffs of smoke were noticed coming up from below decks. By the time she had reached 110th Street, the situation was obvious to all on board and other river craft were sounding warnings. These Schaick seemed to ignore as he plowed ahead with undiminished speed. As he explained later, he was trying to get past the refineries and warehouses lining the banks of the lower East River and make it to Riker's Island where he hoped his burning ship could be beached in comparative safety. Unfortunately, her speed, combined with gusting winds, fanned the flames and soon turned the ship into a floating funeral pyre. She made it to the channel off Riker's Island before being holed on a rock and sinking.

No one really knew how many died, but the death toll was appalling. Official totals ranged from 938 to 1,031, with the higher figure generally accepted. Entire families were wiped out, entire neighborhoods devastated. Scores of victims were never identified and were buried in mass graves.

In the investigation that inevitably followed, a whole series of shocking irregularities were found. Although Captain Schaick was an experienced seaman with a good record, none of his crewmen were experienced or properly trained. Government safety inspections were found to be a joke. To make matters worse, the safety equipment on board the *General Slocum* was, in many instances, useless--or worse. The ship's fire hoses split when crewmen tried to use them. Many of the lifebelts were rotted while others had actually been stuffed by the manufacturer with iron bars in order to bring them up to the official minimum weight! When desperate passengers put them on and jumped into the river, the belts dragged them to their deaths.

Captain Schaick and ten officials of the Knickerbocker Company, the line that operated the *General Slocum*, were indicted for first-degree manslaughter. Only Schaick was convicted. Although at first vilified by press and public, he eventually came to be seen as a victim himself. After all, he was not responsible for the criminal laxity of the government inspectors or of the owners of the steamship line or of the manufacturers of the deadly lifebelts. When those truly responsible walked away scot-free leaving Schaick to bear the full punishment alone, there was widespead public outrage. It was but one more outrage in a hideous tragedy that need not have been.

The photo, above, shows the General Slocum as she must have looked to those boarding her on that June morning. Below, the wreck sunk off Riker's Island. Following pages, the wreck raised. (All photos, Steamship Historical Society/University of Baltimore Library.)

The Saale and the Great Hoboken Fire

Fate often moves in mysterious ways. On the other hand, it--all too often--moves in entirely predictable ways. For example, it generally takes a great calamity, or the immediate threat of a great calamity, to spur governments to take action to protect the public's safety. How long would ships have sailed the seas without adequate life-saving apparatus had not the *Titanic* dramatically proven the cost of that lapse? A steamship named the *Saale* tragically provided another, earlier such lesson one summer day in 1900.

The *Saale*, built in 1886, was a liner of the North German Lloyd line that had its piers across the Hudson from Manhattan, in Hoboken, New Jersey. The NDL, as the line was known, occupied three piers next door to the other great German line, the Hamburg American Line. On the afternoon of June 30th, a fire started in bales of hay being stored on Pier Three, one of the NDL piers. Barrels and casks of flammable substances were also stored nearby. Soon the pier was engulfed in unstoppable flames.

Four NDL liners were present: the crack express steamer *Kaiser Wilhelm der Grosse,* the *Bremen,*

THE BLAZING SAALE IN MID STREAM

Above left, the Saale before the disaster. This photo shows her after her refitting in 1896-97 (Steamship Historical Society/University of Baltimore Library).

Below left, a contemporary postal card depicting the Saale fire. Note the legend at the top: "Doomed men crying for aid out of the cramped portholes."

Above right, another postal card of the era depicting the Kaiser Wilhelm der Grosse during a normal departure from its pier.

Following page, a photo of the unscathed Hamburg American Line pier with the NDL piers in the background. The burned out hulk of the Saale is clearly visible moored to one of the burned out piers (Steamship Historical Society/University of Baltimore Library).

the *Main* and the *Saale*. As winds carried the flames to the other NDL piers, the three ships desperately tried to get up steam and move away from the piers to safety.

The *Kaiser Wilhelm der Grosse* was the first to make it away from the pier and suffered only superficial damage. The others had to be towed from their moorings by tugs hastily called in to assist in the emergency.

A grisly situation soon became apparent as the *Saale* drifted, its decks aflame, in the middle of the river. Those crewmen below decks were unable to make it topside due to the fire raging on the decks and the portholes were too small to permit escape! Those who had been unable to leap for safety into the Hudson River were trapped.

As fireboats drifted helplessly alongside the stricken liner, the desperate victims, clearly visible through the portholes, most screaming, pleading for salvation, succumbed one by one.

It was an experience few who witnessed it ever forgot--and most tried. The final death toll was 99, most of whom need not have died.

The horror of the *Saale* prompted a public outcry for better porthole design. As a result, all liners built subsequently were fitted with portholes of sufficient size to permit a person to escape just the sort of calamity that befell the helpless victims of the *Saale*.

The *Saale*, which sank in shallow water, was later refloated and eventually converted into a cargo vessel. It was finally scrapped in 1924.

The Hoboken piers were rebuilt. And, millions of persons sailed the seas in greater safety.

23

Trouble in Riva Trigoso:
The Launch of the Principessa Iolanda

The moment shipbuilders fear most is that span of a few harrowing seconds as a new ship slides down the ways when the stern is afloat and the bow is still supported by the slip. The middle of the ship is, at that time, totally unsupported and being subjected to stresses it may never again know. The ship is, at that point, also inherently unbalanced, with only the ends supported. Capsizing is a real possibility.

The 9,200 ton *Principessa Iolanda* (sometimes spelled *Jolanda*) was built by Societa Esercizio Bacini at Riva Trigoso for NGI (Navigazione Generale Italiana) and intended for the South American service. Its launch on September 22, 1907 (some sources say it was the 21st), was one of those nightmares that haunt the minds of shipbuilders and ship owners alike.

The *Iolanda* seems to have gotten through the intitial launch phase all right, but then somethimg went terribly wrong and the ship slowly rolled over and sank.

Information on this calamity is very sketchy. It is, in fact, the sort of story that is familiar mostly to dyed-in-the-wool ocean liner buffs. The wreck, incidentally,was scrapped on the spot, right where the *Iolanda* rolled over at the end of the launch ways.

This and following pages, a remarkable series of photos of the launch of the Principessa Iolanda. To the author's knowledge, this is the first time they have been published in book form.

RIVA TRIGOSO-LA NAVE PRINCIPESSA IOLANDA PRIMA DEL VARO

IGOSO - VARO DELLA NAVE PRINCIPESSA I

STAB. CIVICO...
EDIZ. DEPOS...

...IDA – PRINCIPIO DI SBANDAMENTO

RIVA TRIGOSO-VARO DELLA PRIN

SSA JOLANDA - INCOMINCIA LA COMPES

More Trouble at Riva Trigoso: The Principessa Mafalda

Some ships are lucky and some ships are unlucky. This fact is not scientifically provable but the men of the sea have known it since ships were invented. The *Principessa Iolanda* was definitely and unlucky ship, but the *Iolanda's* sister, the *Principessa Mafalda* must have carried the curse, too, because, 20 years after the *Iolanda* rolled over and died, the *Mafalda* did the same thing.

En route from Cape Verde to Rio on October 25, 1927, for NGI, the *Mafalda* broke a propeller shaft. The incoming sea water caused the boilers to explode and the ship began to capsize. Many of the 971 passengers panicked and, in the confusion, 303 perished before help could arrive.

Below, the Principessa Mafalda before her launch at Riva Trigoso, and at sea (Steamship Historical Society Collection).

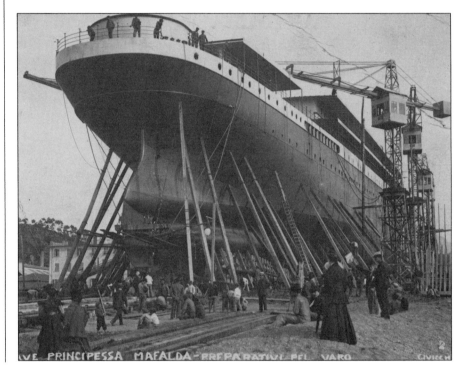

Miracle at the Lizard:
The Salvaging of the Suevic

The treacherous waters off the coast of Cornwall have claimed many victims through the years. That area known as the "Lizard" is particularly feared by seamen so, it was no surprise when, on March 17, 1907, the rocks claimed another ship. This time it was the small combination cargo/passenger ship *Suevic* of the White Star Line.

A 12,000 tonner launched in 1900, the *Suevic* was designed to serve the Australian trade and did so for six years without incident. Hopelessly stranded on Stag Rock in the Lizards, White Star officials gave up all hope of freeing her and called in the salvage experts to see what, if anything, could be done. The advice was unusual, to say the least. Since only the foremost part of the ship was impaled, and since the engines and most of the equipment that constituted the actual value of the ship were aft of that point, why not salvage what could be salvaged and leave the rest stuck on the rock?

Why not, indeed? The *Suevic* was accordingly blown in two just aft of the bridge and the stern portion of the wreck was towed back to Southampton for repairs. Meanwhile, Harland and Wolff, who had built her in Belfast, set about constructing another bow. Soon, the two were joined in drydock and the plucky little *Suevic* continued to ply the seas for another 35 years until, in April, 1942, her crew scuttled her to keep her from falling into Nazi hands.

This and following pages, the wreck and salvage of the Suevic.

WRECK OF THE WHITE STAR LINER "SUEVIC" ON THE TREACHEROUS ROCKS AT THE LIZARD, CORNWALL, MARCH 17TH 19

WRECK OF THE WHITE STAR LINER "SUEVIC" No. 9
REMARKABLE SALVAGE FEAT, AND THE SUCCESSFUL SAVING THE LARGE LINER CUT IN TWO, THE STERN
PORTION BEING TOWED TO SOUTHAMPTON THE BOW PORTION REMAINING ON THE LIZARD ROCKS

Chapter Two

SHIPWRECKS, 1910-1919

The second decade of the century was dominated by the first World War. There were, however, nearly 40 important shipwrecks during the decade involving ships not overtly engaged in war work.

The largest of these was the *Titanic*, on which 1,503 people met their doom. Its sinking after striking an iceberg in April, 1912, has become a modern legend.

The *Lusitania*, torpedoed in May of 1915, was the second in both the size of ship and loss of life. A total of 1,198 persons died off the coast of Ireland when the *Lusitania* went down.

The third worst in both categories was one of the least known great shipwrecks: that of the *Empress of Ireland*, sunk in 1914 in a collision in the St. Lawrence with a loss of 1,014 lives. These three ships are covered in separate sections

After the three mega-disaster wrecks of the *Titanic*, the *Lusitania* and the *Empress of Ireland*--which, among them, accounted for the loss of 3,713 people and more than 95,000 tons of shipping--nothing else that went wrong during this decade seems terribly compelling.

The only important shipwrecks of 1910 were those of the *General Chanzy* and the *Pericles*. The *General Chanzy* was a 2,257 ton CGT liner that was wrecked off Minorca in February with a loss of 93 lives. The *Pericles*, a 10,000 ton Aberdeen Line ship, was wrecked near Cape Town without loss of life.

No ships over 7,000 tons were lost during 1911 and there were only four authenticated deaths. Of interest was the fact that one of the ships wrecked was the *Lusitania*.-- not, however, the *Lusitania*, but, rather, the 5,500 ton Empresa Nacional liner of the same name. Four persons lost their lives when she was wrecked on Bellow Rocks. The second decade of the century thus carries the distinction of being the only one in which two *Lusitania's* sank.

The following year, 1912, was very quiet, too--except, of course, for the wreck of the *Titanic*. The 3,581 ton immigrant ship *Volturno* made the news the next year when it burned in the North Atlantic. It became the focus of a major rescue effort, but 136 people still died.

The year 1914 saw the *Empress of Ireland* tragedy. The *Lusitania*--the *Lusitania*--went down the following year.

In 1916, there were two important wrecks. The fourth largest non-combatant of the decade to come to grief was the 13,000 ton *Chiyo Maru*, of Toyo Kisen KK, was run aground near Hong Kong in March and declared a total loss. There was no loss of life, though. That same month, the 8,371 ton liner *Principe de Austurias*, of Pinillos, Izquierdo y Compania, was wrecked off the coast of Brazil with the loss of 415 lives. In September, 1919, another PIC liner, the 5,000 ton *Valbanera*, was lost in a storm off Cuba. A total of 488 persons lost their lives in that disaster.

There were no other authenticated losses of life in the final four years of the decade and only one ship over 10,000 tons lost other than the *Chiyo Maru*. This was the 10,669 ton *Kristianiafjord* of the Norwegian American Line, wrecked on Cape Race in July of 1917.

Right, the wreck of the Chiyo Maru near Hong Kong (Steamship Historical Society/University of Baltimore Library).

Following pages, North German Lloyd's 10,000 ton Prinzess Irene was beached in a storm off Fire Island in 1911. No one died and the ship was freed (Steamship HistoricalSociety/ University of Baltimore Library).

INZESS IRENE" Ger,
shore FIRE ISLAND BEACH

Collision in the Solent:
The Olympic and the Hawke

Everyone seems aware of the celebrated tragedy that befell the *Titanic*. It is not surprising that the public's attention should have focused on her, but this development represents a dramatic about-face from the situation that existed before the *Titanic* met her doom on that cold April night. A fact people rarely seem to know is that the *Titanic* was only one of three nearly identical sister ships intended to serve White Star routes on the North Atlantic. Not only that, but the *Titanic* was the second of the three.

The *Olympic*, which went into service in 1911, was the first-- hence the designation of the three as "Olympic Class" ships--and it was the *Olympic* that garnered the lion's share of the fame and publicity prior to April 15, 1912. It has been noted by some *Titanic* writers that the *Titanic* went almost unnoticed until she sank. That is perhaps a bit of an exaggeration-- but only a bit and those responsible for the fate of the *Titanic* might have done well to have paid more attention to the problems that befell the *Olympic* early in her career.

The first few voyages of the *Olympic* were uneventful, but disaster struck on the outward bound leg of the fifth. On the morning of September 20, 1911, the *Olympic* departed Southampton with Captain E. J. Smith (who would later command the *Titanic*) as master. Shortly after noon, the *Olympic* was rounding the Bramble Bank at the normal harbor

Above opposite, the Olympic. Below and opposite, the Hawke was able to return to port under her own power.

HMS HAWKE after COLLISION with OLYMPIC - 20 Sept 1911

speed of 19 knots when she encountered the 7,350 ton British cruiser *Hawke*. Both ships turned so as to proceed down the Spithead channel, and, in fact, did so on parallel courses for some distance. They were variously stated to have been 100 to 300 yards apart when, suddenly, the *Hawke* seemed to veer towards the larger ship. A collision was unavoidable and the bow of the cruiser slammed into the starboard side of the *Olympic* about 80 feet from the stern. The bow of the *Hawke* was badly

THE SOLENT COLLISION.
H M S HAWKE RETURNING TO HARBOUR
AFTER THE TERRIFIC IMPACT WITH THE OLYMPIC

smashed and two gashes were left in the side of the *Olympic*, one above and one below the waterline. Remarkably, no loss of life resulted on either ship. The *Olympic* put many of her passengers off by tender at Cowes, then returned to Southampton. Although badly damaged, the *Hawke* made it to Portsmouth under her own power.

The common wisdom was that the cruiser was at fault. The Admiralty put on a strong defense, however, claiming that tests with models demonstrated that the vast difference in displacement of the two ships, and the increasing speed of the *Olympic* as she moved down the channel, had created an irresistible suction that, in effect, dragged the *Hawke* into the liner.

The Court of Inquiry sustained the Admiralty view, although the White Star Line and Captain Smith were held blameless due to the fact that the *Olympic* was under the command of the harbor pilot at the time. The case was eventually appealed all the way to the House of Lords, which upheld the lower court's ruling.

The *Olympic* was returned to

THE SOLENT COLLISION. SEP 11.
WHAT THE HAWKE'S BOWS AND RAM
DID TO THE GT LINER OLYMPIC.
AT THEIR 'MEETING'

Belfast so that Harland and Wolff could effect repairs. The *Titanic* was upstaged as work on her was suspended so that the *Olympic* could be returned to service as soon as possible. The repair work took six weeks. In fact, the fitting out process of the *Titanic* took three months longer than that of the *Olympic* in large part due to the delays caused by the periodic

problems that befell the first of the two sisters.

It was clear from the episode of the *Olympic* and the *Hawke* that even maritime experts had only a

Left and above, the damage to the Olympic was also serious, as these photographs show, although, remarkably enough, no one was killed on either ship.

sketchy idea of precisely how the new class of superliners would perform at sea. Ironically, Captain Smith's experience with the *Hawke* was repeated with *Titanic*, with less graphic results. New ground was being broken and, inevitably when that happens, there were rude surprises in store. How rude those surprises could be, few could conceive at the time.

THE MODERN
MESSENGER OF DEATH:

A typical bearer of the fateful
tidings concerning the "Titanic"

The Wreck of the Century:
The Maiden Voyage of the Titanic

Lord Pirrie, Chairman of Harland and Wolff, and Bruce Ismay, Managing Director of the White Star Line, sat down to dinner one evening in 1907 at Pirrie's Belgravia townhouse in London's fashionable West End. The subject of discussion was the remarkable new Cunard liners, *Lusitania* and *Mauretania*, and the new ships Ismay had in mind to meet their threat.

The dimensions of the proposed ships were astonishing. They were to be 882.75 feet in length, 92.5 feet in beam, have a gross tonnage of 45,000. In contrast, the Cunard giants, the *Lusitania* and *Mauretania*, were some 90 feet shorter, 4 feet narrower in the beam and smaller by over 14,000 tons.

The keel of the *Olympic* was laid down on December 16, 1908. She was launched on October 20, 1910 and completed in May, 1911. The keel of the *Titanic* was laid down on March 31, 1909 and the ship was launched on May 31, 1911. The third of the trio, the *Gigantic*, was to be built later.

Everything about the new ships was on a grander, more

Left, the sinking of the Titanic was front page news all around the world for months. This is the front cover of a typical London picture magazine, The Sphere.

mammoth scale than ever before seen. The *Olympic*, *Titanic* and *Gigantic* were to be composed of eight decks (nine counting the orlop deck). Below the topmost boat deck, the decks were lettered in descent: A, B, C, D, E, F and G. Below G deck were the boiler rooms, holds, etc.

The hulls were to be further subdivided into sixteen watertight compartments by means of fifteen watertight bulkheads, the bulkheads extending up through F deck. Heavy watertight doors provided communication between compartments during normal operation of the ships.

The ships were designed to remain afloat with any two compartments flooded, making them capable of withstanding a broadside collision at any one of the bulkheads. That was just about the worst accident anyone could imagine in ships of this size and the new Olympic Class liners were widely regarded, even by the experts, as being practically unsinkable.

The appearance of the new ships may have belied their size, but 45,000 tons still had to be moved through the water at a substantial pace. Thus, the Olympic Class liners were each to be powered three huge engines with a total shaft horsepower being projected at 46,000. Only in the

horsepower department were the new Cunarders superior. Speed was, after all, the Cunard hallmark and the *Lusitania* and *Mauretania* were each powered by turbines rated at 70,000 horsepower. They were capable of cruising at 26 knots or better. The *Olympic*, *Titanic* and *Gigantic* would be content with 21 knots, not enough to set speed records but still more than competitive.

Turbines were the latest thing and Cunard was switching over to them in a big way. White Star, however, was more interested in economy of operation and came up with a novel three-prop design that used two outboard reciprocating engines with a low-pressure turbine in the middle driving the center prop.

The reciprocating engines were of the four-cylinder, triple-expansion, direct-acting and inverted type. Each engine developed 15,000 horsepower at 75 revolutions per minute (rpm). The low-pressure turbine in the middle was of the standard Parsons type. It developed around 16,000 horsepower at 165 rpm. The elegance of the design was that the center turbine would be run off the excess steam cast off by the reciprocating engines.

Steam to run all this machinery came from no less than 29 huge

boilers. In order to make it easier to work these monster boilers, the double bottom was not continued up the sides of the hull. This particular design compromise would have tragic repercussions.

Twenty lifeboats were fitted to each vessel, 16 of them regular wooden lifeboats and four Englehardt collapsibles. British Board of Trade regulations required ships of more than 10,000 tons to carry 16 lifeboats. This number was woefully inadequate for the number of people, passengers and crew, projected to be sailing on each of the new liners and the Board briefly considered raising the legal minimum to 32, then backed off and let the old regulation stand. Harland and Wolff submitted a proposal for 32 lifeboats anyway, but the White Star Line elected to remain within the standing Board of Trade requirements. In that they were not alone; there was not a single large liner on the North Atlantic with anything like enough boats to handle the evacuation of all passengers and crew.

It is easy, in retrospect, to fault everyone involved. On the other hand, nothing like the *Titanic* disaster had ever happened. None of the people involved at the time had that compelling frame of reference. Moreover, technology is never completely safe. Compromises are inevitable. Atlantic liners had gone from

Left, the launch of the Titanic at Belfast.

Following pages, the Titanic immediately after her launch.

10,000 tons to 46,000 tons in a dozen years and even shipping experts were not fully aware of all the ramifications involved in a change of that magnitude. It was widely believed, for example, that the new superliners were simply too big and too safe to sink.

This leads into another fact, namely that the prevailing view of lifeboats was not the same as ours. We think of lifeboats as being there for the total evacuation of a sinking ship. In 1910, since the experts did not believe the new ships could sink, certainly not suddenly, the lifeboats were there primarily so that people on a stricken ship could be ferried to rescue vessels sure to be waiting nearby in the always crowded North Atlantic shipping lanes. The advent of the wireless radio made this all the more credible. A big ship in trouble would be expected to remain afloat for many hours--even days--with help promptly summoned by radio.

After numerous delays, the *Titanic* was finally scheduled for departure on its maiden voyage on April 10, 1912, with the White Star Line's most honored master, Captain E. J. Smith, in command.

It was almost noon when the *Titanic* began to ease away from the White Star pier at Southampton and depart land for the last time. Disaster nearly struck almost immediately. As the *Titanic* moved majestically through the harbor at a speed of about 6 knots, the steamer *New York* suddenly snapped her moorings and swung menacingly toward the port side. It seemed as if the *Olympic's* collision with the *Hawke* was about to be repeated.

While tug boats frantically attempted to get a line on the wayward American liner, Captain Smith on the *Titanic* first cut his engines, then deftly used the wash from his port engine to halt the swing of the other ship.

The *Titanic's* passenger list included the usual mix of the ordinary and the famous. On board were a total of 2,227 souls, consisting of 1,320 passengers and 907 crew. Several members of the American social register were included, names like Astor, Widener and Thayer. Major Archibald Butt (the Alexander Haig of his day), the trusted friend and advisor to President Taft, was present, returning from an official mission to Europe. Denver socialite, Mrs. J. J. Brown, later celebrated as the "Unsinkable Molly Brown," was there, too--in point of fact, the *Titanic* was how she got the nickname. Artist Frank Millet was on board, as was W. T. Stead, the noted editor, Jacques Futrelle, a noted writer, and theatrical producer, Henry B. Harris. Philanthropist Isidor Strauss was there, too, with his wife Ida. So, too, was industrialist Benjamin Guggenheim. Sir Cosmo and Lady Duff Gordon headed the list of British society. This group brought with it a small army of personal servants, valets, and so on--no less than 31 of them.

Captain Smith himself was something of a celebrity. He was the Commodore of the White Star Line and had been in command of the *Olympic* since she went to sea the year before. At 59, he was due to retire but had accepted the honor of commanding the *Titanic* on her maiden voyage as a farewell gift from the company. It was supposed to be his last voyage for the White Star Line.

The westward voyage from Queenstown was uneventful for the first several days. On Sunday, though, the radio traffic monitored by the Marconi wireless room aft of the bridge began to tell of sightings of ice in the waters a few hours ahead. The *Titanic's* wireless operators even relayed one of these messages to other ships. In all, six warnings had been sent to the bridge, one of which had been given to the captain himself.

At 10 o'clock that evening, the watch on the bridge changed. The new watch crew was headed by First Officer Murdoch, who had

served with Captain Smith on the *Olympic*. Then, at 11:40 the cry came from the crow's nest, "Iceberg right ahead!"

Murdoch instantly took evasive action. He ordered the ship's engines stopped, then called for full speed astern. At the same time, he ordered a hard turn to port. For what seemed an eternity, the ship bore inexorably down on the iceberg. It took perhaps half-a-minute before she slowly began to answer the helm, but the turn had only just commenced when her 46,000 tons slammed into the looming wall of ice.

Captain Smith appeared on the bridge almost immediately after the collision and, taking charge, ordered various officers and crew members to reconnoiter for a damage assessment. When the damage reports started coming back a few minutes later, the news was chilling. At least five--and possibly six--of the *Titanic's* watertight compartments were taking water. The inflow might be

Many of the big wigs associated with the *Titanic* were present for the maiden trip. J. Bruce Ismay, Managing Director of the line, was there. So, too, was Thomas Andrews who ran Harland and Wolff for Lord Pirrie and had overseen the building of the ship.

Above, the Titanic in the fitting-out area at Belfast.

Right, the old liner New York with which the Titanic nearly collided at Southampton.

contained by the pumps in one or two of those compartments, but the *Titanic* was only designed to float with two compartments flooded. Thomas Andrews, who had also made his way to the bridge at the first sign of trouble, offered his grim expert's opinion on the reports: the ship was doomed.

Meanwhile, many passengers were unaware that a collision had taken place. Even those who felt the crash and had seen the iceberg brush by doubted the seriousness of the situation. Of course, as the list of the ship became more and more pronounced, it became progressively easier to find takers for the boats. Even then, however, the officers in charge refused to fill them. They were afraid the boats would buckle if loaded to their rated capacity. It wasn't until the last 45 minutes or so, when only a handful of boats remained, that they were sent down the sides with anything like their full capacity.

At 12:15, Captain Smith ordered his wireless operators to begin sending distress messages. Another tantalizing possibility was presented by a ship apparently sitting five or ten miles away on the horizon. The officers on the bridge of the *Titanic* could see what looked like a light or lights, but

The Olympic and Titanic set new standards for comfort on the North Atlantic. The photos on this page give ample proof of that. Clockwise from the bottom left, the a la carte restaurant, the second class library and the first class smoking room.

Following pages, one of the last photos taken of the Titanic, as she departed from Southampton for New York.

had no idea who it was. This was the ship most experts now believe to have been the Leyland liner, *Californian*. Smith had the wireless room try to reach it. There was no response. He ordered the morse lamp to be used from the bridge. Still, no response. Around 12:45, the first of the *Titanic's* distress rockets were fired. Over the next hour-and-a-half, a total of eight rockets were sent up in a final desperate attempt to reach the mystery ship, but the ship never responded.

Other ships were taking notice, however; the *Titanic's* wireless distress calls had been picked up by a number of liners. One of the ships was fairly close, at only 58 miles: the 13,564 ton Cunard liner *Carpathia*. The *Carpathia's* captain, Arthur Rostron, gravely read the wireless message from the *Titanic*, then sprang into action. Without a moment's hesitation, he ordered his ship turned around and headed at full speed toward the *Titanic's* stated position.

Meanwhile, on board the *Titanic*, the situation was growing progressively worse. As the bow sank lower and lower into the dark Atlantic, then, finally, disappeared from view around 1:15, the passengers and crew began to come to terms with their individual fates. For a fortunate few, there

S.S. Titanic. Starting on maic
April 10th Wrecked on an i
April 14th 1912 whose con

voyage from Southampton
off Cape Race and sunk.
882 feet.
Beken

First Class Lounge Promenade

Corridor Private Suite Promenade

Bath Rooms

First Class Dining Saloon

Companion way Stairs Second Class

Third Class Dining Saloon

Water Line

Boiler Room

ICEBERG
From 50 to 100 feet
according to various
accounts

← Starboard port holes

were seats in the lifeboats. Others jumped into the icy water in anticipation of the end, clinging to whatever they could, hoping to make it to one of the lifeboats. Most, however, remained behind in the deceptive security of the sloping decks.

It was almost possible to believe that the ship would somehow survive. The lights still shone brightly; in fact, it seemed as if every light on board the ship was brilliantly aglow. In the first class smoking room, drinks were "on the house." On an upper deck, the orchestra continued to play, featuring a selection of cheerful tunes. Only the creak of the remaining lifeboats being lowered in their davits and the relentless advance of the black waters up the sloping decks predicted the horror that was about to ensue.

At 2:05, the last lifeboat departed. At 2:17, the stern suddenly rose into the air until it was nearly vertical against the starlit sky. As it did so, the freight and anything else movable broke loose all at once and fell toward the bows with a tremendous, thundering crash. As this transpired, the lights on board flickered and went out, then came on again in an eerie red glow, then flickered out for the last time. The stern of the ship then stood like a

Left, this is how the London magazine, The Sphere, imagined the actual collision.

Following pages, The Sphere's artist's conception of the Titanic's final minutes complete with quotes from survivors.

black, sinister finger pointed heavenward and hung in that incredible position for at least a minute before settling back slightly and disappearing from view. It was 2:20 a.m.

The ensuing cries of those 1,500 souls struggling in the frigid waters formed the most heart-rending and nightmarish sound ever heard, continuing for perhaps an hour, slowly diminishing as the victims one-by-one succumbed to their fate. Throughout that time, not one lifeboat returned to help.

The first, tentative rays of dawn were creeping over the eastern horizon when the *Carpathia* approached the *Titanic's* radioed position. When the light of day finally distinguished sea from sky, all that greeted the *Carpathia* was a pathetic little fleet of lifeboats. Of 2,227 people on board, only 705 survived the night.

Almost as soon as the *Titanic* disappeared into the black waters of the North Atlantic 350 miles southeast of Newfoundland, people began talking of salvaging the wreck. The most daunting obstacle was simply finding it.

In 1985, spurred by the development of advanced sonar technology and remarkable deep-diving robot submersibles, a joint U.S.-French expedition set out to do the impossible. The search used the *Alvin* submersible developed in 1964 by the Woods Hole Oceanographic Institution in co-operation with the U.S. Navy. On September 1, 1985, the search succeeded. The American team, under the direction of Dr. Robert Ballard, finally discovered the

wreck of the *Titanic.*

The ship is broken into three parts. There are two main sections. One consists of the forward half of the ship. The other comprises the final third, measuring forward from the stern. That leaves perhaps 15-20% of the ship missing in the area of the third and fourth funnels. Part of this third section has reportedly been located, but not thoroughly explored. The bow and stern sections, however, have been exhaustively photographed and studied.

The bow section is in relatively good shape. The funnels are missing and much of the wood has been eaten away, but the hull and superstructure are essentially intact. The stern section, on the other hand, is in severely damaged condition and lies some distance away from the forward section with the stern turned around so that it points in the same general direction as the bow. Between the two sections lies a debris field. No human remains have been found.

Will the wreck of the *Titanic* ever be salvaged? It is feasible--and therefore possible--that items from the wreck may someday be salvaged, despite an active international campaign to prevent such activity. The wreck lies in international waters and is legally fair game. It seems highly improbable that the wreck itself will be brought up. It is simply too far down and in too many pieces to make any attempt to do that seem worthwhile given current technology. Still, if the *Titanic* has taught us anything, it is that nothing is impossible.

"The Titanic looked enormous"

Boat Deck clear of boats →

"The bows & bridge completely under water"

...se Floating Ice

"Sea calm as a pond There was just a gentle heave"

Above, the Carpathia.

On this page and opposite, various contemporary souvenirs of the sinking. It has been well-documented, incidentally, that the orchestra did _not_ play "Nearer My God to Thee"--in any language!

Calamity on the St. Lawrence:
The Sinking of the Empress of Ireland

When one thinks of the perils of the deep, one naturally conjures up images of lonely expanses of water, of sudden and ferocious storms, of icebergs lurking in the darkness in the middle of the vast reaches of the sea. One probably does not think of cruising down a river in a large and modern passenger liner only a few thousand feet distant on either side from terra firma. Well, perhaps one should rethink one's fears. Perhaps one has not heard of the *Empress of Ireland*.

Built by Fairfield Shipbuilding and Engineering in Glasgow, the *Empress of Ireland* and her sister, the *Empress of Britain*, were 14,000 ton liners commissioned by the Canadian Pacific for the lucrative North Atlantic trade. In the case of the CPR, that meant Quebec to Liverpool by way of the St. Lawrence River.

The two new *Empresses* were essentially identical and fit squarely within the CPR tradition of handsome ships. Indeed, if the CPR ever built an ugly ship, this writer has not yet seen the picture. Some of the CPR liners for the more exotic Pacific trade were extravagantly stylish, sporting clipper bows and wildly raked funnels--just the thing to cruise the Mysterious East. Those ships built for the North Atlantic tended to be more staid, although almost without fail of splendid proportion and line.

The *Empress of Ireland* was launched on January 27, 1906, and completed on June 7th of that same year. The maiden voyage, from Liverpool to Quebec, began on June 29th. She was a large ship by the standards of the time; at 14,191 tons, she was fully 60% as big as the White Star Line's *Adriatic*, the largest ship in the world when launched later that year. Moreover, while never intended to be a record breaker, she was a fast ship. Her 19,000 hp quadruple expansion engines were capable of delivering enough power to her twin screws to propel her at a more-than-respectable 18-20 knots. Finally, she was a comfortable ship. The CPR built a solid reputation on the unostentatious comfort of its liners. The *Empress of Ireland* was designed to accommodate 310 first class passengers, 350 second class and 800 in third.

On the 28th of May, 1914, the *Empress of Ireland* departed Quebec for Liverpool with 1,057 passengers. Of these 87 were in first class, 253 were in second class and 717 were in third. Shortly after 1 o'clock in the morning, Captain Henry Kendall dropped off the river pilot at Father Point, near Rimouski, then proceeded toward the mouth of the St. Lawrence and the open sea.

Approaching the *Empress*, coming upriver, was a Norwegian collier, the *Storstad*, under the command of First Mate Alfred Toftenes. The *Storstad* was carrying 11,000 tons of coal to Quebec. As soon as the two ships sighted one another's lights in the early morning darkness, the sort of confusion that was to doom the *Andrea Doria* some 42 years later came in to play. Each misjudged the course and speed of the other ship. Each took action to ward off danger that, in practice, had the opposite effect. The situation was grievously complicated by the fact that no sooner had they sighted one another than the river was suddenly engulfed in a blanket of fog. Now effectively blind, the two ships groped toward each other in the goo taking whatever evasive actions their respective bridge crews hoped would avert calamity.

Captain Kendall was by far the more worried of the two men in command that night. When the fog rolled in, he stopped his engines, then reversed them in order to--he

The card reproduced, right, was typical of sort of sentimental "Bon Voyage" cards sent to-or-from loved ones in this era. It is the sheerest coincidence--and irony--that the ship they selected was the Empress of Ireland.

thought--put more space between the *Empress* and the unknown ship approaching upriver. Unknown to him, the *Storstad* was proceeding on a course that assumed the continued forward progress of the *Empress* on a course different from that she was actually taking. When the collier's captain, Thomas Andersen, arrived on the bridge in response to the suddenly thick weather, the first thing he saw was the starboard side of the *Empress* looming out of the fog, directly ahead. About the same time, Captain Kendall saw the lights of the *Storstad* coming toward him. Kendall frantically ordered "full speed ahead," while his horrified counterpart on the *Storstad* ordered engines full astern. For both, it was too late. The bow of the *Storstad* plowed into the side of the liner, nearly cutting her in two.

Captain Kendall realized at once that his ship was doomed and commenced every possible effort to evacuate his passengers as quickly as possible. In that laudable goal, he was, unfortunately, fighting against bitter circumstance. In the first place, most of his passengers--and many of the crew--were asleep in

Left, the crumpled bow of the Storstad. Compare this to the damage done to the bow of the Hawke when she struck the Olympic. The angle and location of a blow makes a huge difference. One of the little known facts about this tragedy: 20 persons lost their lives on the Storstad, so the collier did not emerge from this human tragedy totally untouched.

their bunks below decks. To compound this, it was the first night at sea and most of the passengers were unfamiliar with the ship, or, indeed with their own cabins, so moving quickly was a problem. To make matters even worse, the collision quickly knocked out the electrical system so that those below decks were left totally in the dark. Add to all that the fact that the *Empress* capsized in barely 10 minutes, and it is easy to see why 80% of the passengers never saw the dawn of a new day. It was later estimated that, depending on his location in the ship, a passenger had anywhere from no chance at all to no more than several minutes to leave his cabin and get above decks. Many passengers were, literally, drowned as they slept.

After the *Empress* capsized, she lay on her beam ends for a short time--accounts vary on this point, but it was probably about four minutes--sinking lower and lower into the water. In one of the most poignant recollections to come out of a shipping disaster, a passenger from Winnipeg named Cunningham wrote about those final minutes as the *Empress* lay on her side, almost flush with the surface of the river, while hundreds of frightened people clung to her hull:

The boat did not seem to be sinking. The water was just creeping up. The side was at a gentle angle with the water. It was just like sitting on the beach watching the tide come in. The waves came splashing

up the slope of steel, and then retired one after the other. But each came a little higher than the last.

Then, with a final convulsion, her stern rose into the air and she took her final plunge to the river bottom 150 feet below. The *Empress of Ireland* was no more.

The magnitude of the disaster was truly staggering. Of 1,057 passengers in all classes, only 217 survived. The crew did a bit better, largely because relatively more crewmen were up and about when the *Storstad* struck, but, even so, 172 crewmen died out of a compliment of 420. Thus, the death total was 1,012, making this the third worst regularly scheduled passenger liner disaster of the century overall, and the <u>worst</u> in numbers of passengers lost, exceeding both the *Titanic* and the *Lusitania* in this latter category. That this story is not better known by the general public is probably due more to the location than anything else. The big New York-bound liners got most of the glory in life and, even in death, a liner in the Canadian service found it tough to break into the big time.

The Canadian inquiry cleared Captain Kendall and found the Norwegian ship entirely at fault in the catastrophe. The Norwegians were incensed at this, however, and held their own inquiry in response, finding the CPR vessel at fault! Whomever was at fault, the 1,032 men, women and children (from both vessels) drowned in the cold, black waters of the St. Lawrence paid the price.

Turning Turtle in Chicago:
The Eastland Disaster

If the *Empress of Ireland* sinking ranks as the unknown among great ocean liner wrecks, the *Eastland* disaster must rank as one of the least known calamities of the century among passenger ships in general. Recently, the *Chicago Tribune* reported that officials of the Illinois Historical Society had never even heard of the wreck, despite the fact that it happened in Chicago and still today ranks as the worst single human disaster in Illinois history.

The *Eastland* was one of a number of well-known passenger excursion ships operating on the Great Lakes. She had a reputation for being a "tender" ship; she did not ride well in rough weather because of an excessive amount of superstructure. In other words, she was top-heavy. Still, the *Eastland* worked the lakes successfully for a number of years.

On the morning in question, July 24, 1915, the *Eastland* had been chartered by the Western Electric Company for an employees' picnic. The *Eastland* was to embark the employees and their families--the vast majority of whom were from suburban Cicero--at her pier near the Clark Street Bridge on the Chicago River. It was subsequently estimated that some 2,500 persons had boarded. This was far too many and one explanation later offered was that only adults had been counted as the employees boarded. A significant percentage of those boarding were,

For an unknown disaster, there is an amazing amount of material available on the Eastland. This writer has turned up several full-color advertising cards of the ship and numerous photographic cards illustrating various stages of the rescue work that went on. This comparative wealth of material contrasts sharply with the General Slocum, similar in service and time period, upon which there seems to be virtually nothing.

The wonderful color illustration, opposite, was just a Chicago scenic postal card, but what a wonderful depiction of the Eastland. The card, below, is an authentic Eastland advertisement.

Following pages, various photos of the rescue work from the hours and days after the sinking.

however, children. To make matters worse, many passengers headed for the upper decks which, given the excessive numbers on board, only served to exacerbate the inherent top-heaviness of the passenger ship.

Soon after the *Eastland's* engines were started, she suddenly heeled over and capsized right there in the Chicago River next to her moorings. Most of the victims never had a chance.

It was thought at first that as many as 1,500 might have died, but the official total eventually set the figure at 812. The toll was especially devastating because it was concentrated among families in one community. A reported 22 families were completely wiped out by the disaster. Another 600

families lost at least one member and the entire city of Cicero was numb with shock and grief. Almost everyone had lost a friend, neighbor or relative.

As for the *Eastland*, she was salvaged and--minus her top-most deck--placed back in service, although not as a passenger carrier. In that guise, she served without notable mishap for many more years, all-but forgotten.

In Chicago, an historical marker has finally been erected at the site of the disaster, only the ninth historical marker in Cook County, Illinois. Remarked Patricia Gibbs, the historical marker supervisor for the State of Illinois, "We'd never heard of it. It's just amazing."

It is amazing, indeed.

EASTLAND. ALL STEEL AND STRICTLY FIREPROOF.

S.S. Eastland, after disaster
Chicago Rive

MAX STEIN-CHI.

EASTLAND
DISASTER   8 AM JULY

Above top, the Franconia.
Above center, the Laconia, Above
bottom, the Ivernia.

Above right, the Campania
(Steamship Historial Society/
University of Baltimore Library).

The second decade of the century was dominated by the first World War. This war erupted in August of 1914 and dragged on for another four years. There were tremendous losses to shipping, primarily as a result of the submarine mining and torpedoing activities of the German Navy.

The *Lusitania*, flagship of the Cunard Line, was the most famous victim of this policy despite the fact that she was not overtly engaged in military activity at the time of her sinking. This event caused a

Victims of Total War:
Liners Lost in World War I

firestorm of criticism in Britain and America and was a major factor in turning American public opinion toward war.

Tragic as her loss was, however, the *Lusitania* was not the largest passenger ship lost during the decade. Indeed, at 31,000 tons, she was not even close. The 46,000 ton *Titanic*, sunk in 1912, was half again as big. Nor was the *Lusitania* the largest passenger ship lost during the war. The 48,000 ton *Britannic* took that unfortunate prize. The *Britannic*, one of the two sisters of the *Titanic*, was not only the largest loss in the British merchant marine during the war, she represented a crippling blow to the White Star Line from which that line arguably never really recovered. The 32,000 ton *Justicia*, torpedoed in the last days of the war in July, 1918, was bigger than the *Lusitania*, too. It was being built as the Holland-American Line's *Statendam*, but was commandeered by the Admiralty for war work, much as was the *Britannic*.

Other important passenger liners were lost during the war, as well. Most of these included ships engaged in combatant roles of one kind or another. They included the *Franconia, Ivernia, Laconia, Campania* and *Carpathia* of the Cunard Line, the *Britannic, Cymric, Laurentic* and *Afric* of the White Star Line, the *La Provence* of the CGT and the North German Lloyd liner, *Kaiser Wilhelm der Grosse*.

This was "total war," as it came to be known, and the great ocean liners were obviously not immune to its destruction. Even for those that survived, the going was rough. The wartime career of the *Olympic* is extremely instructive in that regard.

The only one of the three great White Star sister ships to complete a peacetime voyage, the *Olympic* survived some difficult early experiences to become the Grand Old Lady of the North Atlantic, plying the sea lanes for nearly a quarter-of-a-century. At the time of her building, she was the largest liner in world. She lost that honor for the few days the *Titanic* was in service, then regained it until the German *Imperator* (later expropriated by Cunard as the *Berengaria*) was completed in 1913. She was the largest British-built liner until the *Queen Mary*.

The outbreak of war on

August 4, 1914, found the *Olympic* on her way to New York. She completed that voyage, then switched from Southampton to Glasgow for the British terminus and continued commercial voyages for several months.

As there was very little eastbound traffic, much of this time was spent ferrying an estimated 6,000 American nationals from the war zone back to New York. It was on one of these voyages that the first of her

R.M.S. "OLYMPIC." 46,359
(The largest British Steamer
Viewed from a Seaplane while on War S

war adventures occurred.

Passing Lough Swilly off the coast of Ireland, the *Olympic* happened upon the British battleship *Audacious* just after the latter had struck a mine. The *Audacious* was a new ship of the King George V Class and displaced 23,000 tons, making her about half the size of the *Olympic*. The *Olympic* stopped to render

The remarkable photo, left, of the foundering Audacious was probably taken from the Olympic.

Above, the Olympic trooping, resplendent in her dazzle paint.

assistance, a humanitarian action that, in retrospect, was probably rather stupid. Her master not only risked brushing into any one of the unknown number of mines in the area, but, for the duration of the rescue, she was a sitting duck for any passing German submarine-- and a fabulous prize at that. Her luck held, though, which is more than could be said for the unfortunate battleship. The *Olympic* took off most of the warship's crew then attempted to take her in tow. Due to heavy seas, however, the tow was unsuccessful and the *Audacious* sank. The Admiralty imposed a news blackout on the whole incident and even went so far as to confiscate film from passengers on the *Olympic*!

The *Olympic* was commissioned as a naval transport in September, 1915. In this guise, she made four trips to the Mediterranean in connection with the Dardanelles and Gallipoli campaigns. Late in the year, she was attacked by an enemy submarine but was able to use a combination of speed and evasive maneuvers to escape unharmed.

In February, 1916, the *Olympic* was attacked twice again by enemy submarines and twice again emerged unscathed.

In March, 1916, she was returned temporarily to the White Star Line. During this period, she was fitted with six 6-inch guns for submarine defense. In April, 1916, the *Olympic* was chosen to host an important British diplomatic mission to the United States. The delegation, headed by A. J. Balfour, was delivered to Halifax, Nova Scotia, then returned from the United States to Britain.

For the rest of the war, the *Olympic* was engaged in trooping duties, bringing American and Canadian fighting men to the war front. For this service, she was "dazzle" painted (see the illustration in this chapter). Dazzle painting was a fairly bizarre tactic used to ward off submarine attacks by (hopefully) rendering ships optically untrackable. That was the theory, at least. It is not recorded whether it worked against competent submariners--and the

Above top, the Afric.
Above center, the Cymric.
Both ships were White Star liners.
Above bottom, the President Lincoln, built by Harland and Wolff (like the Afric and Cymric), had started out as a Hamburg America Line ship. Interned in New York during the war she was seized by the U.S. Government for trooping. All three ships were torpedoed during the war.

Top, the White Star liner, Laurentic, subject of one of the greatest salvage operations in history. Sunk in a minefield off Northern Ireland in 1917, the 14,800 ton liner was carrying £5,000,000 in gold. Of the 475 persons on board, 354 perished and resulting the salvage

operations to recover the gold lasted until 1924.

Center, the Royal Edward was torpedoed on August 14, 1915, in the Aegean with the loss of 935.

Bottom, the Minnetonka in heavy seas. Both this ship and her sister, the Minnehaha were lost to German torpedoes.

tactic was not revived by the British during World War II--but while it lasted it certainly made for uniquely colorful ocean travel!

In May, 1918, during its twenty-second trooping voyage, the *Olympic* met her greatest adventure of the war. She was attacked by German submarine U-103. The torpedo was avoided by quick evasive action, but then the *Olympic* did a remarkable thing. She turned on her attacker and rammed it! Actually, the blow to the submarine was described as "glancing," but even a light blow from a 46,000 ton ship is quite a wallop and the submarine immediately began to sink. Some of the German crew managed to escape and were picked-up by a passing American destroyer.

By the end of the war, in November, 1918, the *Olympic* had compiled an impressive record in service to the Allied cause. Without casualty, she had transported 41,000 civilian passengers, 66,000 troops (two-thirds of them American, the rest Canadian), and 12,000 members of a Chinese labor battalion--119,000 people in all. In so doing, she steamed a grand total of 184,000 miles, burned 347,000 tons of coal and survived four known attacks by enemy submarines. She proudly carried the affectionate nickname, "Old Reliable."

During the first part of 1919, the *Olympic* repatriated thousands of troops to the New World. That finished, she returned to Harland and Wolff for a $2,430,000 refurbishing and refitting for postwar commercial service.

Luck or Duplicity?
The Sinking of the Lusitania

The 31,550 ton *Lusitania* was one of a pair of mammoth liners commissioned just after the turn of

Opposite and below, early advertising illustrations of the Lusitania. The two sisters were almost always advertised as a pair and even after the Lucy was lost, the Cunard Line continued for years to use favorite Lusitania illustrations, simply redubbing them, "Mauretania."

the century by Cunard. The other was the *Mauretania,* and, between them, the two sisters were certainly among the most famous liners of all-time--if not the most famous. Except for a near fatal fire at Southampton in 1921, the *Mauretania* led a charmed life, held the Blue Ribband speed trophy for many years and was retired in 1935. The *Lusitania,* the first of the two, seemed headed in a similar direction until it bought a German

torpedo early in World War I.

The *Lusitania* was torpedoed off the coast of Ireland on the afternoon of May 7, 1915, by the German submarine (U-Boat) *U-20.* The precise location was the Old Head of Kinsale, within sight of the Irish coast. The single torpedo blast was followed seconds later by a tremendous explosion from within the ship and she soon developed a drastic list to starboard. Within 20 minutes she

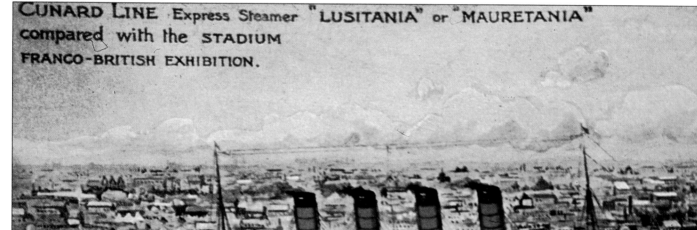

CUNARD LINE Express Steamer "LUSITANIA" or "MAURETANIA" compared with the STADIUM FRANCO-BRITISH EXHIBITION.

was gone. Of the 1,959 people on board--including 440 women and 129 children--1,198 perished, making this the third worst disaster of the century involving a scheduled liner. Public opinion was outraged in Britain and America and the sinking laid the groundwork for popular support for America's eventual entry into the war on the Allied side.

Controversy has, however, dogged the *Lusitania* disaster. There have for years been assertions in print and elsewhere that the *Lusitania* was engaged in the secret transportation of war material for the British, including explosives. This is one possible explanation for the speed with which she sank, although the ignition of the coal dust by the initial torpedo blast would explain it just as well (and was probably the cause for the sinking of the White Star liner *Britannic* in similar circumstances in the Aegean in 1916). The British initially insisted that there were two torpedoes, an assertion contradicted by the U-Boat's log (and other evidence) and a cause of much unhelpful confusion over the years.

Other writers have gone even further and stated that Winston Churchill, then First Lord of the Admiralty, deliberately exposed the *Lusitania* to peril in hopes that her sinking would help bring America into the war--which, of course, it did. Conspiracy theories aside, this writer leans to the belief that it was a coal dust explosion, although the transport of contraband by the *Lusitania* is also highly probable. It seems incredible that Churchill would have ordered such a fate for one of Britain's greatest ships and, in fact, more than 70 years after the fact, no convincing documentary evidence to support such a position has surfaced.

Ironically, Lord Mersey was the Wreck Commissioner for all three of the greatest ocean liner disasters of the century: the *Titanic*, the *Empress of Ireland* and the *Lusitania*. There is pretty clear-cut circumstantial evidence to support the view that he railroaded Captain Turner of the *Lusitania*. This is another fact that has fueled conspiracy theories. It does not mean, however, that the sinking was a deliberate, calculated set-up by anyone--including the German

U-Boat commander, who seems to have pretty much lucked into the biggest kill of the war.

The steamship companies were, not surprisingly, experts at touting their services to prospective passengers. The original brochure issued by Cunard for the *Lusitania* and *Mauretania* makes fascinating reading--particularly the claim that the new ships are unsinkable. Part of that brochure is quoted below:

"The CUNARD LINE unrivaled for the *safety* with which it has carried its thousands upon thousands of passengers, now offers to its patrons the 'Lusitania' and 'Mauretania,' the safest, fastest, most magnificent steamships in the world.

"The history of this oldest

Previous pages, the Lusitania under full steam at sea.
Opposite, B-Deck and the second class smoking room.

Above, the second class drawing room.
Below, the Lusitania docked at the landing stage in Liverpool.

Liner at Landing Stage, Liverpool

1st Class Dining Saloon,
S S LUSITANIA.

Transatlantic Steamship Company has been one of steady progress. From a beginning with the 'Britannia,'--the finest vessel of her day--a primitive paddle wheeler of 1154 tons; 740 horse-power, carrying 100 passengers at eight and a half knots, the development of the present fleet has been gradual but striking.

"Each link in the chain--the transition in construction from wood to iron and from iron to steel; the evolution from the paddle wheel through all phases of single and twin-screw reciprocating engine driven vessels to the quadruple-screw turbine-propelled express steamers 'Lusitania' and 'Mauretania,' the last word in naval architecture and having no equal in the world; the development of wireless telegraphy and submarine safety-device signalling--each has represented

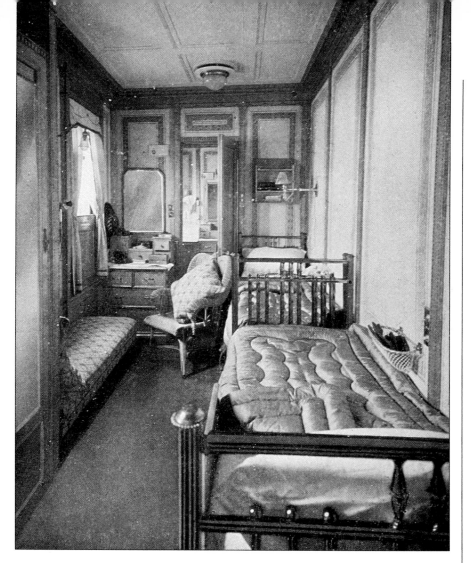

Opposite, luxury in the first
class dining saloon and the first
class lounge.

Above, a comfortable first
class cabin on A-Deck.
Below, the Veranda Cafe.

'something better' than ever before existed, and each has marked an epoch in over-seas travel.

"Limitation of language makes adequate word description of these mammoth Cunarders impossible. Of special design, in equipment and passenger accommodation they are constructed on similar lines. The following figures show their immense dimensions: Length, 790 feet; breadth, 88 feet; depth, to boat deck, 80 feet; draught, fully loaded, 37 feet 6 inches; displacement on load line, 45,000 tons; height to top of funnels, 155 feet; height to mastheads, 216 feet. The hulls below draught line are divided into 175 watertight compartments, *which make them unsinkable* [author's italics]. With complete safety device equipment, including wireless telegraph, Mundy-Gray improved method of submarine signalling and with officers and crews all trained and reliable men, they are unexcelled from a standpoint of safety as in all other respect.

"Size is however their least remarkable feature. Each ship is propelled by four screws rotated by turbine engines of 68,000 horse-power capable of developing sea speed of more than twenty-five knots per hour regardless of weather conditions, maintaining without driving a schedule with the regularity of a railroad train, and thus establishing their right to the title of 'fastest ocean greyhounds.'

"The passenger accommodation throughout, for 550 first-class; 500 second-class; and 1300 third-class, is no less wonderful, and in magnificence

and comfort is unapproached.

"Size and height of saloons and private staterooms, combined with exquisiteness of design, sumptuousness of decoration, and fitted with every modern electrical device tending to comfort, including telephonic communication with every part of the vessel, make it impossible to realize that they are rooms aboard ship.

"Regal suites, consisting of two bedrooms, private dining room and butler's pantry, reception room and bathroom, are adorned with delicate tapestries; furnished with Sheraton dressing tables, brocaded settees, bedsteads of brass, and fitted with the best of bedding, blankets and linen-the whole cared for by skilled fingers.

"There are open fireplaces; windows shaped and curtained; nooks and cozy corners and even elevator service conveniently located to make inter-deck communication a pleasure.

"Heating and ventilating an important feature, has received the attention deserved-the improved thermotank system, of proven scientific excellence being used.

"Sanitary lavatories, bathrooms and showers, in white tile and enamel are numerous, conveniently distributed and amply supplied with hot and cold water at all hours.

"The Cunard cuisine, famous for excellence, needs no commendation, and special attention is paid to the a la carte service where one may dine at any desired hour or give private dinners without extra charge.

"The following photographs were taken on the "Lusitania" sailing from New York, September 16,1908...in strong N.N.E. and S.W. gales, with high, heavy rough confused seas, showing that in *steadiness,* as in every other respect, they are the 'unexcelled.'"

Above, this card was issued at the time of the sinking and expressed all too well popular feeling in Britain and America. Entitled, "The Last Plunge," the copy on the back read,"The last sight of the famous vessel, the pride of the whole kingdom; one more victim, the worst of all of German Kultur. One more atrocity to add to the number which makes the whole German nation stink in the nostrils of all Christian nations." There weren't many in either camp who were neutral on the issue of submarine warfare.

Opposite, America was by no means united on the war, however. This ad ran after the war and expressed the pacifist sentiment that was growing and that would find full flower in the isolationist movement 20 years later.

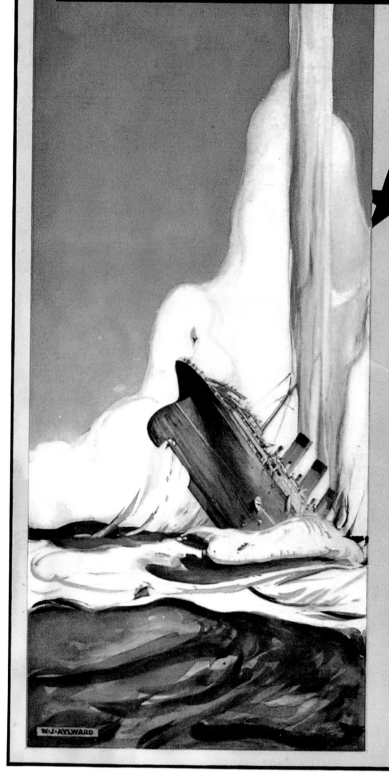

SO THE LUSITANIA WENT DOWN

Well, what of it?

★

"What of it?" you cry. "The whole world was shocked. For days the newspapers talked of nothing else."

Well, but what of it? After all, it was a little thing.

How many Lusitanias would have to go down to carry all the dead and missing soldiers and the dead civilians of the great World War?

One Lusitania a day.
For a year.
For 10 years.
For 25 years.
For 50 years.

One Lusitania a day for 70 years, or one a week, beginning nearly a century before the discovery of America by Columbus and continuing to the present hour.

That is the number of Lusitanias that would be required to carry the dead. The dead of all nations who died in the war.

This advertisement, written by Bruce Barton, painted by W. J. Aylward and presented here through the co-operation of FORTUNE and the courtesy of the AMERICAN MAGAZINE, is the first exhibit of an educational campaign dramatizing the horrors of war; a campaign which Henry Ewald has called "a bold, practical plan which dwarfs all former use of advertising." Co-operation to develop this campaign into a persistent, extensive, efficient drive for Peace is invited by World Peaceways, Hotel Roosevelt, Madison Avenue at Forty-fifth Street, New York City.

The Titanic's Unknown Sister:
The Wreck of the Britannic

Most people who know of the *Titanic* (and nearly everyone does these days) are surprised to learn of the existence of the first of the three sister ships, the *Olympic*. When you tell them about the third

Previous pages, the H. F. Alexander (ex-Northern Pacific) on the beach at Fire Island. Formerly, the Northern Pacific was one of the fastest liners in the Pacific service.

Below, the brochure issued at the Britannic's launch in 1914.

of the trio, the *Britannic*, and how she suffered a tragic fate almost as catastrophic as that of the *Titanic*, they are incredulous. This is yet another disaster ship of which no one seems ever to have heard.

The third of the White Star Line's unlucky trio was launched in February of 1914, too late to go into service as a commercial liner before the outbreak of war. The British Admiralty decided she should be completed as a hospital ship. Fitting out as a passenger

ship would have to come later (and, as it turned out, never).

The *Britannic* was slated to be the third member of the triad begun by the *Olympic* and *Titanic*, to provide the White Star Line with 46,000 ton weekly departure capabilities from both New York and Southampton. As such, she was intended to be similar to the first two.

The designs of the three ships would have been much closer still had it not been for the *Titanic*

WHITE STAR LINE

ROYAL
AND
UNITED STATES
Mail Steamer

"BRITANNIC"
(TRIPLE SCREW)

LAUNCHED AT BELFAST
26th February 1914.

Above, a White Star rendering of how the Britannic would have looked in service.

Below, the Britannic on the ways ready for her launch.

disaster, an event which forced a major rebuilding of the *Olympic*. Work was suspended on the *Britannic* (or *Gigantic* as she was originally called!) and numerous design changes were made before work was restarted.

The alterations in the *Britannic* made her the largest in gross tonnage of the three: at 48,158

tons, she was about 5% larger when fitted as a hospital ship and probably would have been about 50,000 tons (about 10% larger) when fitted as a commercial liner.

Most of this was due to the vastly increased internal compartmentalization, to the giant-sized lifeboat davits, to somewhat heavier construction throughout and to a whole list of safety gear and redundant systems. Following the *Titanic* debacle, the White Star Line was obsessed with safety.

Accommodations were projected for 2,500 passengers and 950 crew. The facilities in the *Olympic* and *Titanic* were improved upon, particularly in first class with more private baths and the addition of a fourth elevator.

Artist renderings of the proposed interiors show them to have been a bit more ornate than those on her sisters. The Promenade Deck, which was entirely open on the *Olympic*, was enclosed for about one-third of its length on both the *Titanic* and the *Britannic*. In addition, the Well Deck on the *Britannic* was also enclosed, and was another factor which increased tonnage. Tonnage is based on enclosed space, not weight *per se*, as the term implies.

The *Britannic* was requisitioned by the Admiralty on November 13, 1915, and officially completed as a hospital ship by December 12th. While on a trip from Salonika on November 21, 1916, she was sunk in the Kea Channel in the Aegean.

The explosion took place on the starboard side shortly after 8 a.m. and she went down in about

55 minutes. The explosion apparently occurred at the watertight bulkhead between holds #2 and #3. The bulkhead separating holds #2 and #1 was also damaged. At the same time, boiler rooms #5 and #6 began taking water. Thus, the area of damage was roughly the same as that sustained by the *Titanic* four-and-a-half years earlier.

The magnitude of the damage was revealed by Jacques Cousteau in an expedition in 1976. The ship is lying on her starboard side in about 375 feet of water and her hull below the Shelter Deck is completely blown away at the bulkhead separating holds #2 and #3. The hull and sections of the keel simply aren't there for a distance of perhaps 60-70 feet! The bow section remains attached to the rest of the ship primarily by the upper decks. The port side hull plates are bent outward, indicating a tremendous explosion from inside the ship. The best guess is that the mine or torpedo struck her in the reserve coal locker igniting the coal dust.

The captain, Charles Bartlett, stayed at his post until all on board had been sent away in the 35 lifeboats lowered. Rescue vessels were on the scene in several hours. Of more than 1,100 on board, only 30 died. Another 45 were wounded. Most of the deaths reportedly occurred as the ship remained underway when two port lifeboats were launched prematurely and were sucked into the still turning screws. As a strange footnote to the tragedy, one of the crew members, Violet

Jessup, had been a member of the crew on the *Titanic*! She survived both sinkings.

There was considerable controversy over whether she had been sunk by a mine or by a torpedo. The channel had supposedly been cleared of mines the day before and there were reports of submarine sightings in the area. Still, the naval board of inquiry was unable to reach a conclusion either way.

It all seems rather academic in retrospect and the best evidence is that it was a mine, but a torpedo would have pleased many. Torpedoing a hospital ship would have been yet another example of the wickedness of the Hun and one more propaganda tool for the British cause.

The lingering question

surrounding the *Britannic*--and one never adequately addressed in the inquiry that followed--was how a ship designed--over-designed, in some ways--for safety, as was the *Britannic*, could have sunk so quickly, if, indeed, at all. The damage was similar to that of the *Titanic*, yet the *Titanic* (without all the structural alterations that went into the *Britannic*) remained afloat nearly three times as long.

It has been speculated that the watertight doors may not have been closed. That would seem to be an act of criminal negligence for a ship sailing in a combat zone in wartime and really is hard to conceive. It is possible that the damage was more extensive than anyone has ever discovered. This remains one of the fascinating mysteries of the sea.

Above, the Britannic as she looked when fitted out as a hospital ship. Closer to the Titanic in appearance than to the Olympic (although the three were sisters)

the Britannic can be distinguished most easily by her out-sized lifeboat davits.

Below, the launch of the Britannic in February, 1914.

Chapter Three
SHIPWRECKS, 1920-1929

After the mayhem of the second decade, the century's third decade almost had to be an improvement. There were only a score of important passenger liner wrecks between 1920 and 1929 and only three of them resulted in significant loss of life. Moreover, there were two entire years without any major wrecks at all. Ironically, the worst wreck came before the decade had hardly begun.

On January 20, 1920, the 5,407 ton Chargeur Reunis liner, *Afrique*, was wrecked off the Bay of Biscay. Engine trouble was the culprit, combined with high winds and heavy seas that forced the helpless ship on the rocks of the Roche-Bonne Reefs and prevented nearby ships from rendering assistance. Of 585 passengers and crew on board, 553 perished. Later the same year, the 8,500 ton *Bohemian* of the Leyland Line was wrecked off Nova Scotia. This time there were no fatalities.

In 1921, the only calamity of note was the burning of the 10,000 ton Allan liner, *Grampion*, at Antwerp. There was no loss of life. In May, 1922, 86 people died when the 7,912 ton *Egypt*, of the P&O Line, sank following a collision off Egypt. Two 10,000 ton ships were wrecked that same year without loss of life: The *Wiltshire* was wrecked off New Zealand, while the *City of Honolulu* (formerly the *Friedrich der Grosse*) burned off California.

In April, 1923, 23 persons died when the 4,600 ton *Mossamedes*, of Empresa Nacional, was abandoned off Angola. A month later, the 11,000 ton *Marvale*, of the Canadian Pacific Line, was wrecked near Cape Race with no loss of life.

Remarkably, there were no major wrecks during 1924 or 1925 and there was only one major ship

Below, the Vestris.

98

Above, the Afrique (Steamship Historical Society/University of Baltimore Library).
Below, the Celtic.

wrecked in 1926, Messageries Maritimes *Fontainbleau*, burned out at Djibouti with no fatalities.

The sole major wreck in 1927 completed a sorry tale. It involved the *Principessa Mafalda*, the sister ship to the only major liner that ever sank at its launching: the *Principessa Iolanda*. On the 25th of October, 1927, while off the coast of Brazil en route to Rio, the ship capsized taking 303 of her 1,259 passengers and crew to their deaths. (See page 34.)

The two big stories of 1928 were the *Vestris* and the *Celtic*. *Vestris* was a 10,000 ton Lamport & Holt liner that served South American routes. On November 10th it left New York. It already had a noticeable list when it left port, probably due to improper cargo loading, and the list became

progressively worse as the ship proceeded down the American coast in heavy weather. By all accounts, the captain, W. J. Carey, was grossly slow to appreciate the danger and, when he did, it was too late to either save the ship or summon assistance before the *Vestris* rolled over and sank. Of 326 passengers and crew, 112 died in the sinking or in the water before help arrived. Captain Carey chose to go down with his ship.

The 20,000 ton White Star liner, *Celtic*, which at one time had been the largest ship afloat, was

wrecked a month after the *Vestris* went down. While attempting to enter Queenstown Harbor during a 70 mph gale, she was blown onto the rocks at Roche's Point. The 254 passengers--25 of whom were survivors of the *Vestris* disaster!-- were taken off safely. The *Celtic*, however, was delcared a total loss.

Also in 1928, the Chargeurs Reunis liner, *Cap Lay*, was lost in a typhoon in the Bay of Along. It is not known how many persons died in that tragedy.

There were no passenger liner calamities of note in 1929.

Chapter Four
SHIPWRECKS, 1930-1939

The 1930s were the years when everything seemed to catch fire. Of 27 notable shipwrecks involving important passenger liners, there were a dozen that burned, with well over 200,000 tons of shipping destroyed. Remarkably enough, only 217 persons were reported to have died in all of these fire catastrophes and most of them perished on one ship: the *Morro Castle*.

Of all the ships that came to grief during the 1930s, the *Morro Castle* is the only one still remembered by many people in North America. The real story for the maritime industry, however, was the series of catastrophic fires experienced by the French steamship companies. Four of the most important passenger ships in the French merchant marine were destroyed in the process. One of these French ships was the second passenger liner this century to sink on its maiden voyage. Another was the second largest passenger liner ever destroyed in regular service.

The first year, 1930, saw five

Previous pages, the City of Honolulu burns at Honolulu (Steamship Historical Society/ University of Baltimore Library).
Right, the City of Honolulu.

wrecks, but only three involving ships of more than 10,000 tons and only two recorded losses of life. The first ship to go was the 13,900 ton *Monte Cervates*, of the Hamburg-South America Line. It was wrecked on January 22nd in the Straits of Magellan with the loss of one life.

In May, the *City of Honolulu* burned. The *City of Honolulu* had started life as the Hamburg America Line's *Kiautschou* (1900-1904) and later sailed as the *Prinzess Alice* for North German Lloyd (1904-1917). After being taken as a war prize, she was kicked around for a while until finally returned to service as the *City of Honolulu* for the Los Angeles Steam Ship Company on the Los Angeles-to-Honolulu run. On May 25, 1930, she was gutted at her pier in Honolulu but was able to return to Los Angeles under her own power. She was deemed too old to repair, however, and was scrapped by 1933.

The third major ship to sink or be wrecked in 1930 was the 14,000 ton *Highland Hope*, of the Nelson Line, which was grounded in a fog on the Farilhoes Rocks on a voyage to Buenos Aires. The one fatality was a passenger who panicked and jumped overboard.

The following year, 1931, was quiet until the 19,000 ton Furness liner *Bermuda* burned at Hamilton, Bermuda, on June 17th. The fire was put out but, later that same day, she caught fire again, this time with one fatality. Again the

fire was put out, but now the ship had to be sent to the U.K. for repairs. While under-going them, she caught fire for a third time and was completely gutted. Sent to the breakers, she went on the rocks en route and was declared a total loss.

Another ship that seemed unable to avoid fire, was the 14,000 ton *Pieter Corneliszoon Hooft*, of the Nederland Line. Launched in 1926, she was gutted while still being fitted out. Repaired, she sailed for several years in the Far East service until she caught fire at the Sumatra Quay in Amsterdam on November 14, 1932, and was destroyed.

The other disaster in 1932 was that of the 17,000 ton *Georges Philippar* of Messageries Maritimes. She caught fire during her fitting out and was repaired. Preparing to leave on her maiden voyage to Yokohama, she was the subject of anonymous threats reported by French police. On the return trip, she caught fire in the Gulf of Aden and was destroyed. Between 40-90 persons died, depending on the source. Arson was suspected.

In 1933, the second largest liner ever wrecked in regular service met her doom. This was the *L'Atlantique*, flagship of the Compagnie de Navigation Sudatlantique, caught fire on January 4, 1933, while en route to Le Havre and became a total loss. (See pages 108-113.) Seventeen crewmen lost their lives in the confusion.

In 1934, there were two major wrecks. On June 20th, the *Dresden*, a 14,000 ton North German Lloyd liner, was wrecked off Norway with a loss of 4 lives.

The big news story in 1934, however, was the *Morro Castle*. On September 8th, the 11,000 ton Ward Line flagship burned off the coast of New Jersey with a loss of 137 lives. The wreck washed ashore at Asbury Park and became an instantaneous tourist bonanza. (See pages 114-117.)

In 1934, the Cunard and White Star companies were merged by under pressure from the British Government with the Cunard Line very much the senior partner. Almost immediately, the White Star fleet began to be liquidated. Fabled ships such as the *Olympic* and *Majestic* were soon sold or scrapped. On Sepember 5, 1935, 16,000 ton *Doric* was involved in a collision off Cape Finisterre with the 2,000 ton, French steamer *Formigny*. Although all the passengers were got off safely and the *Doric* made it to port under her own power, it was decided that she was uneconomical to repair and she, too, was sent to the scrappers. Also in 1935, the 13,000 ton *Ausonia*, of the Societa Italiana di

Servizi Maritimi, burned, at Alexandria with a loss of three lives and was declared a total loss.

Nineteen thirty-six passed without notable shipwrecks until October, when the Spanish Civil War intruded. The 10,000 ton *Cristobal Colon*, of the Compania Transatlantica Espanola, was comandeered by Spanish terrorists and accidentally wrecked off Bermuda, the first of three notable acts of terrorism involving liners this century. (See pages 128-129.)

The two American flagships in the Pacific were the 21,000 ton *Presidents Hoover* and *Coolidge* of the Dollar Line. On December 10, 1937, the *President Hoover* was wrecked off Formosa. No lives were lost but the ship was declared a total loss. (See pages 118-119.)

The following year, 1938, was another disastrous one for fires. On May 4th, the 25,000 ton *Lafayette*, of the Cie Generale Transatlantique (French Line), and the largest French motorship on the North Atlantic, burned at Le Havre and was a total loss. In August, the 19,000 ton *Reliance*, of the Hamburg American Line, burned

at Hamburg and was also declared a total loss.

The situation hardly improved in 1939, on April 19th, the French Line's 34,000 ton *Paris* burned at Le Havre, probably due to arson. No one died, but the wreck remained in the harbor until after the war when the *Liberte* (ex-*Europa*) ran into it and sank. At that point, officials finally got around to scrapping the remains. The *Liberte* sank on an even keel, fortunately, and was refloated.

The first victim of World War II was the 13,000 ton Anchor-Donaldson liner, *Athenia*, torpedoed, off Ireland with a loss of 112 lives.

The final shipwreck of note in the fourth decade of the century was the 12,000 ton *Cabo San Antonio*, of Ybarra y Cia. The *Cabo San Antonio* burned in the South Atlantic with loss of five lives after a devastating fire broke out in the galley.

The 1930s had been a tough decade for passenger shipping. Unfortunately for the world, unimaginably worse times were just over the horizon.

Opposite bottom, the Pieter Corneliszoon Hooft.

Opposite top, the Art Deco interior of the Paris (Steamship Historical Society/University of Baltimore Library).

Center top, the Paris (right) and the Ile de France.

Above right, the burning of the Cabo San Antonio (Steamship Historical Society/University of Baltimore Library).

Right top, the Lafayette and, bottom , the Queen of Bermuda.

Following Pages, the wreck of the Paris in Le Havre at war's end. This photo is from a scrapbook of snapshots taken by the author's father in late-1944 or early-1945. There is bomb damage visible, too.

— Paquebot "l'ATLANTIQUE".

Art Deco Disaster:
The Burning of the L'Atlantique

The *L'Atlantique* is virtually unknown to all but confirmed ocean liner enthusiasts. This is probably due to the fact that she served in the less visible South American service and to the fact that she was only in service for about 15 months. She was built by Penhoet in St. Nazaire, the same people who commenced the fabled *Normandie* a few months later, and went into service for Cie Sudatlantique in September of 1931. She measured 42,512 tons and was designed to carry 1,156 passengers and a crew of 663.

The *L'Atlantique* was the largest ship ever to call at South American ports and served as a prototype for the spendors that were to come on the fabled *Normandie*. Indeed, the interiors of the *L'Atantique* are so similar in some cases as to be *Normandie*

108

look-alikes at a casual glance, although on a smaller scale.

The *L'Atlantique* was also the second largest passenger liner in regular service ever lost, exceeded only by the *Titanic*. The *Seawise University* (ex-*Queeen Elizabeth*)

Right, some of the interior splendors for which this ship became famous: the bedroom of a de luxe suite, top, and the private dining room, center, that came with it. Below, the stunning chapel on board the ship.

The public rooms left little to be desired. Left top, the first class Salon Ovale and, bottom, the first class Grand Salon. Below, the "piece de resistance," the first class Salle a Manger--or dining room--almost a Normandie prototype.

Following pages, the burning of the L'Atlantique.

was not yet in service and the *Normandie* had been taken over by the U. S. Navy.

The *L'Atlantique* was on the way to Le Havre from Bordeaux without passengers and with a reduced crew on January 4, 1933, when she caught fire. The fire started in an unoccupied stateroom and quickly spread throughout the ship. The ship was, at that point, 22 miles away from the Isle of Guernsey. Within four hours the crew was forced to abandon ship. Nineteen crewmen died.

The *L'Atantique* drifted afire in the English Channel for two days before being met by ocean-going tugs and towed to Cherbourg. The Cie Sudatlantique then got into a brawl with the insurers who wanted to accept a bid from Harland and Wolff to refit her. The line wanted her abandoned. The line eventually won and what was left of the splendid *L'Atlantique* went to the breakers in 1936.

The Hulk of Asbury Park: The Burning of the Morro Castle

The *Morro Castle* and the *Oriente* were nearly identical 11,520 ton turbo-electric liners built for the Caribbean service of America's Ward Line. This was in the days when Havana was a tourist destination of preference for Caribbean-bound Americans. A Ward Line booklet assured curious travelers of what they would find:

"So here we are in Havana, and here you may be, baking biscuit-brown on the strand of this delicious winter-time resort after a brief, comfortable trip. The day begins auspiciously; all days begin auspiciously in Havana..."

The *Oriente* had a normal, unremarkable career, but the *Morro Castle* was destroyed in a celebrated fire that made headlines through out the world and, half-a-century after the fact, continues to arouse interest because of the spectacular and mysterious features of the wreck.

The trouble began on the evening of September 7, 1934, when the captain of the Morro Castle was found dead in his cabin. Although the cause was apparently natural, the ship was now under the command of a crew that was clearly not up to the responsibility. Indeed, it included one man who was probably a borderline psychotic who has been fingered by numerous writers and researchers as the man who, in all likelihood, started the fire so he could play "hero." With the most experienced man on board--the

COOL CRUISES to HAVANA

$65 SEVE[N] DAYS MINIMUM • INCLUDING ALL EXPENS[ES]

WARD LINE

captain--now out of commission, the fire, which was discovered in the early morning hours of September 8th, quickly raged out of control.

At this juncture, the *Morro Castle* became a sort of ocean-going version of the *General Slocum*. The superstructure was entirely ablaze within half-an-hour and the bridge had to be abandoned. Fortunately, an SOS had been sent just before the wireless room was engulfed in flames, but that was the only cheery note of the morning. Six lifeboats were launched and were filled primarily with crewmen, which gives pretty good idea of the level of competence on board the *Moro Castle* in that regard.

The *Monarch of Bermuda*, the *City of Savannah* and the *Andrea F. Luckenbach* answered the *Morro Castle's* distress call and picked up a total of 158 survivors. Another 150 were rescued by fishing vessels in the area and by Coast Guard vessels that rushed to the scene. The final death total was put at 133.

The Coast Guard attempted, unsuccessfully, to take the *Morro Castle* in tow. Instead, the smoldering wreck washed ashore at Asbury Park, New Jersey, at around 7 o'clock that morning. There it quickly became a magnet for the curious. The city fathers reportedly considered buying the wreck and in order to keep it on as a tourist attraction, but those

plans were abandoned and the *Morro Castle* was eventually carted off the the breakers.

The saga of the *Morro Castle* was, however, the big shipwreck of the 1930s for Americans. It remains today one of the few shipwrecks about which the public has any significant awareness.

Below, a colorful brochure issued by the Ward Line to advertise their $65, seven-day excursions to Havana. The brochure trumpeted: "Never a dull moment in any of your precious vacation days." How true!

Following pages, the wreck of the Moro Castle, still smoldering, after washing ashore at Asbury Park, New Jersey.

ummer Vacation Cruises to Havana on the

MOUS "*MORRO CASTLE*"
·E·L·

S.S. MORRO CASTLE

SHORE AT ASBURY PK

The Dollar Line's Disastrous Duo: The Presidents Hoover and Coolidge

The Dollar Line was the American passenger line that made the biggest splash during the 1930s in the Pacific and the *Presidents Hoover* and *Coolidge* were the flagships of the line. Built by Newport News Shipbuilding and Drydock Company, the 21,936 ton *Presidents* were in many ways oversize versions of the *Morro Castle* and *Oriente*, which were also Newport News ships. Each was designed to carry 988 passengers and a crew of 385 and both entered service in 1931.

Disaster first struck the *President Hoover*--or, rather, the *President Hoover* struck a reef near Formosa (Taiwan) en route from Kobe to Manila. The date was December 10, 1937.

The passengers and crew were gotten off but all subsequent efforts to refloat the ship were unsuccessful. In the summer of 1938, the wreck of the *Hoover* was sold to Japanese breakers and scrapped on the spot.

Disaster befell the *President Coolidge* five years later, after the Dollar Line had folded and after the opening of World War II. She had been requisitioned for trooping work by the United States Government in 1941, even before the outbreak of war. On October 26, 1942, the *Coolidge* was transporting some 5,000 troops from New Caledonia to Espiritu Santo. Because of poorly communicated instructions to her bridge, she entered the harbor through the wrong channel and found herself in a minefield. Her captain attempted evasive action too late. Fortunately, she sank on a relatively even keel and was evacuated with a remarkably low loss of only five men.

The wreck of the *Coolidge* was never scrapped and still lies in the harbor of Espiritu Santo. It is just about all that remains of the ambitious Dollar Line.

Opposite, an original Dollar Line rendering of the Presidents Hoover and Coolidge. The two sisters were virtually identical in appearance.

Right, the President Coolidge (Steamship Historical Society/ University of Baltimore Library).

Below, the President Hoover stranded on the rocks. There were several unsuccesful attempts to refloat the Hoover, but, in the end, the rocky shoals won out over man's best efforts (Steamship Historical Society/University of Baltimore Library).

Chapter Five
SHIPWRECKS, 1940-1949

The fifth decade of the century was clearly dominated by the world war. Among other things, World War II proved the greatest calamity to befall shipping since the development of the boat as a means of transportation. Major passenger liners lost during the war included the cream of the Italian, French and German lines, virtually the entire Japanese passenger fleet and several important Canadian, British and American liners for good measure.

Italian war losses included the *Rex*, the 51,000 ton flagship of the Italian Line, and the *Conte Di Savoia*, between them the two greatest Italian liners of the century. The premier French loss was the greatest of all French liners, the *Normandie*. German losses included the *Columbus* and the *Bremen*. The Canadian Pacific liner, *Empress of Britain*, considered by many to be among the most beautiful liners of the century, was an early casualty of the war and the greatest among the British Commonwealth losses. The American losses were headed by the *President Coolidge*, America's largest ship in the Pacific service.

World War II cost the world much more than beautiful ships, however. The war was responsible

for several of the greatest losses of life at sea. Three disasters vie for the dubious honor of being the worst shipwreck in all history: the *Lancastria*, the *Cap Arcona* and the *Wilhelm Gustloff*. Incredibly, as many as 20,000 people may have died on these three ships. Some sources contend the total was higher than that. The worst, by common consensus among researchers who track that sort of thing, was the *Wilhelm Gustloff*.

Despite the dominance of the

Opposite, the Magdalena (Steamship Historical Society/ University of Baltimore Library).

Above, the Manhattan stuck off the coast of Florida in 1941. She was pulled free (Steamship Historical Society/University of Baltimore Library).

war in the disaster listings, there were a couple of notable civilian calamities. The first came in January, 1940, when the 14,000 ton *President Quezon* (ex-*President Madison*), of the Philippine Mail Line, wrecked off the Riukiu Islands in Japan. There were no reports of causalties, but the ship was scrapped.

The probable second of three episodes of terrorism involving passenger liners occurred later that year. On November 25th, the 11,000 ton Messageries Maritimes liner, *Patria*, was waiting at Haifa to embark on a voyage to Palestine with 1,900 emigrants. The ship was sunk by three explosions and 279 persons died. Those responsible were never found.

The next significant passenger liner disaster did not transpire until

April 25, 1949, when the 17,000 ton *Magdalena*, of the Royal Mail Line, was wrecked off Rio de Janeiro on her maiden voyage. Thus, the *Magdalena* became the third ship this century to be wrecked on her maiden voyage and joined the *Titanic* and the *Georges Philippar* in that category. Remarkably, Harland and Wolff, in Belfast, built both the *Magdalena* and the *Titanic*. Unlike the *Titanic*, however, there were no fatalities when the Magdalena went down.

So, it was the best of times and it was the worst of times. It was the worst of times for passenger ship losses and for fatalities. Nearly all , however, were war-related. There were only two civilian disasters and no fatalities, making this decade the safest for regular ocean travel.

121

Le Paquebot « NORMANDIE »

Chinese Fire Drill:
The Destruction of the Normandie

The *Normandie* is regarded by many steamship enthusiasts as being the greatest ocean liner of all-time. At 79,280 tons (later expanded to 83,423 tons) she was not quite the largest liner ever, but she was an Art Deco palace the likes of which the world has never seen. There were many who loved her and a few who thought her garish, but she was undeniably unique in the history of shipping.

The *Normandie* was built in the same St. Nazaire yards of Penhoet that had built the *L'Atlantique*. Launched a few weeks before the *L'Atlantique*

burned in the English Channel, the *Normandie* went into service in May, 1935, for CGT (Companie Generale Transatlantique). At that time she was the largest ship in the world--a prize she narrowly wrested from the *Queen Mary*--but was exceeded by the *Queen Elizabeth* in 1940.

And she was fast. The *Normandie* won the Blue Ribband from the Italian liner, *Rex*, on her maiden voyage with a recorded speed of just over 30 knots. The award was won, in turn, by the *Queen Mary* in 1938 (and, eventually, by the *United States*,

which has held it for almost four decades and, considering the deplorable state of affairs in the ocean liner business these days, may never be challenged).

The fame of the *Normandie*, however, was in her decor. She was exuberantly, extravagantly decorated, a masterpiece of French 1930s design. A key feature was the sheer size of her main rooms. The first class dining room formed a vista that seemed as wide as a football field and just went on and on into the distance as far as the eye could see. This was, of course, calculated, the result of

F R E N·C H   L I N E

assures you of Luxury...Speed...Safety...Cuisine

Travel via French Line is unsurpassed in every detail of luxurious living. Our whole fleet (manned and officered by hardy Breton and Norman seafarers) averages less than 7 years in service. The NORMANDIE . . . largest and fastest liner in the world . . . is a revelation in beautiful decoration and modern streamlining . . . maintaining and further developing the high tradition of the ILE DE FRANCE. Your Travel Agent will be glad to make reservations without charge.

BEDROOM—FÉCAMP SUITE—THE NORMANDIE

SALON—CAEN SUITE—THE NORMANDIE

French Line

610 FIFTH AVENUE (ROCKEFELLER CENTER), NEW YORK CITY

To England and France direct, and thus to all Europe : NORMANDIE, April 22 • ILE DE FRANCE, April 4 • PARIS, April 11 • CHAMPLAIN, May 2 • LAFAYETTE, April 18

French Line

STEAMER _____ DATE _____

NAME _____

CABIN _____

PTD. IN U.S.A.

FROM A COVERED PIER AT NEW YORK TO A COVERED PIER AT HAVRE

124

*Above, the Normandie backs
out of her pier in New York
(Steamship Historical Society/
University of Baltimore Library).*

*Below, the swimming pool (or
"piscine," a word that sounds
vaguely distasteful in English).*

*Opposite above, the giant
doors leading into the first class
dining room. Opposite below, a
French Line luggage sticker.*

NORMANDIE" LE HAVRE · SOUTHAMPTON · NEW YORK

ingenious engineering: the uptakes to the funnels were split and ran up the sides of the ship, permitting unbroken vistas of interior space.

The *Normandie* was laid up at New York in late-1939 in order to protect her from the Germans. When France fell in 1940, her position became increasingly uncertain and, on December 12, 1941, she was finally seized by the U. S. Government. Work soon began to convert her into a navy troop transport to be renamed the *Lafayette*. On February 9, 1942, a welder's torch started a fire that soon consumed the superstructure. New York fire officials responded by pumping so much water into her upper decks that she became unstable and, the following day, rolled over onto her side at the pier. Mortally embarassed, the navy set about salvage work which succeeded after 17 months. By then, however, it was late in the war and conversion work was never resumed. She was scrapped soon after the end of the war.

Above, a Normandie card.
Right, the burned-out hulk
(Steamship Historical Society/
University of Baltimore Library).

Terrorism on the High Seas:
Not As Recent As Most Believe

Terrorism has become a modern curse, with hijackings, assassinations and simple, cold-blooded murders of non-combatants a depressingly common occurrence in many parts of the world. When the *Achille Lauro* was hijacked in 1985, most people assumed that it was the first time ever that a large passenger ship had been so victimized. Alas, there have been at least three significant episodes this century.

The first occurred during the Spanish Civil War. The 10,000 ton *Cristobal Colon*, of the Compania Transatlantica Espanola, was commandeered either by Spanish leftists or Spanish rightists (accounts differ on this point!) and accidentally wrecked off Bermuda on October 24th.

The probable second of three episodes of terrorism involving passenger liners occurred in 1940. On November 25rd, the 11,000 ton Messageries Maritimes liner, *Patria*, was waiting at Haifa to embark on a voyage to Palestine with 1,900 emigrants. The ship was sunk by three explosions, taking the lives of 279 persons. Those responsible were never brought to justice.

Finally, the *Achille Lauro* (ex-*Willem Ruys*) was hijacked on October 8th, 1985, while cruising between Alexandria and Port Said off the coast of Egypt. Most of the passengers were ashore when the hijacking occurred, but one American passenger was murdered, his body thrown overboard. On October 9th, the hijackers surrendered to Egyptian authorities who agreed to turn them over to the PLO. The hijackers were, in turn, hijacked by American armed forces, however, with their getaway plane forced down at an American base in Sicily. An international uproar followed that and the Italian Government fell as a direct consequence.

Above, the Cristobal Colon (Steamship Historical Society/ University of Baltimore Library).
Opposite, the Achille Lauro (ex-Willem Ruys), the most recent incident of terrorism on a liner.
Opposite inset, the Patria.

Disasters of World War II: Item One, The Lancastria

The *Tyrrhenia, Tuscania California* and *Cameronia* were 16,000 ton sisters built for the Anchor Line right after the end of World War I. All four ships were around 578 feet in length (although the *Cameronia* was lengthened considerably to increase her stability) and all were fitted with 13,500 hp geared turbines capable of moving them through the sea at 16-17 knots. The *Cameronia*

Lancastria in the London-to-New York service until the worldwide economic depression reduced business on that run sufficiently that other uses had to be found. So, from 1932 on, the *Lancastria* was used almost exclusively for cruising service. Finally, the *Lancastria* became a troop transport early in 1940.

On June 16th of that year, during the final rout of Allied forces just prior to the capitulation of France, the *Lancastria* was embarking persons at St. Nazaire as part of the general evacuation of Allied forces from the continent. On June 17th, while waiting at St. Nazaire for the formation of its convoy, the *Lancastria* was attacked by German aircraft, experienced four direct hits, and sank in about 20 minutes.

Official figures placed the numbers of those on board at around 5,500, with a death total estimated at 2,500. The Association of *Lancastria* Survivors in Britain contends that the total was deliberately underestimated by the British Government and that the actual numbers on board were around 9,000, of whom only 4,000 survived. Whatever the actual figures, they were certainly staggering.

One of the *Lancastria's* old sister ships, the *California*, had some trouble, too. She was attacked by German aircraft in July, 1943, while trooping in a convoy west of Oporto, caught fire and was abandoned with a final death toll of 46.

Above, the Lancastria.

made her maiden voyage in 1921 and *Tyrrhenia* entered service in 1923. Initially, she was used in the Canadian service, making the run from Glasgow to Montreal. In 1923, the ship was switched to London-to-New York service. Then, in 1924, the *Tyrrhenia* was transferred to the Cunard line and renamed the *Lancastria*.

Originally designed to carry 265 passengers in first class, 370 in second class and 1,150 in third with a crew of 320, Cunard decided to combine first and second classes into the new "cabin class." Passenger accommodations then stood at 580 cabin class and 1,000 in third.

Cunard continued to use the

S.S. "CERAMIC"

Disasters of World War II: Item Two, The Ceramic

The 18,713 ton *Ceramic* was not the largest loss of life during the war, nor was she the largest ship lost. The interest in the *Ceramic* lies in the unusual circumstances of her death.

the Mediterranean, she was fired upon by a submarine--deck gun, not torpedo--and chose to do battle until the ridiculous relic of a gun she had (it had been lifted from a Japanese cruiser, circa 1887) jammed. At that point, she cut and ran at what observers estimated at 25 knots. That rate of speed was impossible, but there can be no doubt the *Ceramic* was suddenly in a hurry to be somewhere--anywhere--else!

In 1917, she encountered another submarine while, according to records, carrying a load of bullion to South Africa. Why the *Ceramic* would have been carrying *gold* bullion to South Africa is a mystery (perhaps it was soup). At any rate, she avoided the torpedo and went on her way.

In 1934, the *Ceramic* was transferred to Shaw, Savill & Albion. Then, in 1940, she was taken over by the British Government as a troop transport.

On December 7, 1942, while travelling from Australia to Britain with 656 people on board, the *Ceramic* was torpedoed by German submarine *U-515* off the Azores. The attack occurred just after midnight and the explosion was so catastrophic that no SOS could be got out and the ship sank almost at once. In fact, only one man lived to tell about it and he was picked up by the submarine and interned as a prisoner of war! Thus, it was quite a long time before the Admiralty even learned what had happened to the *Ceramic*.

Above, the Ceramic in her White Star colors.

At the time she entered service, the *Ceramic* was the largest liner in the important Australian service and remained so for many years. The *Ceramic* was the largest ship of the old White Star Line sunk during the war (if you discount the *Georgic*, which was refloated and returned to service).

Ironically, the *Ceramic* had had some exciting moments in World War I, as well. In 1916 while in

134

Disasters of World War II: Item Three, The Cap Arcona

The 27,560 ton *Cap Arcona* was built in 1927 by Blohm & Voss for the Hamburg-South America Line. She was designed to accommodate 1,315 passengers and 630 crewmen. Her maiden voyage from Hamburg to La Plata occurred on November 19, 1927.

On November 19, 1940, the *Cap Arcona* was taken over as an accommodation ship by the German Navy at Gotenhafen and served in that capacity until the final days of World War II. In the early months of 1945, she was pressed into service to help evacuate the Eastern Front from the threat of the advancing Red Army. Some 26,000 persons were evacuated in three voyages.

In April, 1945, some 5,000 concentration camp prisoners were taken on board at Neustadt. There were, at that point an estimated total of some 6,000 persons on board in all.

On May 3rd--mere days before the end of the war in Europe--the *Cap Arcona* was attacked by British aircraft. The ship quickly capsized and an estimated 5,000 lives were lost--the vast majority of them prisoners whose liberation might have been only days, or even hours, away.

The sinking of the *Cap Arcona* was surely one of the cruelest ironies of the war. After the cessation of hostilities, she was broken up on the spot.

Left, the Cap Arcona.
Below, some of the first class public rooms on the Cap Arcona.

Disasters of World War II: Item Four, The Wilhelm Gustloff

Above, the Wilhelm Gustloff while still under construction.

Below, one of five saloons on board the Wilhelm Gustloff.

The *Wilhelm Gustloff* was one of a fleet of ships projected to be built for the German Government, the Nazi Party and various and sundry branches and organizations affiliated with each. The *Wilhelm Gustloff* was managed by the "Kraft durch Freude" (Strength Through Joy) organization that was also responsible for the development of the Volkswagen car (originally the KdF Wagen, or Strength Through Joy Car).

The *Wilhelm Gustloff* was a 25,484 ton ship built by Blohm &

Voss. She was launched in 1937 and completed in March, 1938. She was designed for 1,465 passengers--all tourist class--and a crew of 426. According to published reports at the time, the North German Lloyd organization was put in charge of operating the ship on her cruises, which were to be mostly to Norwegian fjords.

After serving as a hospital ship and, later, as an accommodation ship during the war, the *Wilhelm Gustloff* was pressed into service evacuating the Eastern Front early in 1945. On January 30th, she was torpedoed in the Baltic by a Soviet submarine. Although help arrived quickly, she capsized in about an hour. Only 904 persons were rescued. The question is: How many died? Some records say that 6,100 were on board, while others put the figure as high as 10,000. Whatever the actual total, it seems probable that the *Wilhelm Gustloff* holds the unenviable record for taking the greatest numbers of people to their deaths in a single shipwreck.

Right top, a view of the two-berth cabins that were used throughout the ship. The Wilhelm Gustloff was a one-class worker's ship and, as such, was intended as a comfortable, rather than luxurious, ship in terms of her fittings and accommodations.

Right center, more views of a typical two-berth cabin.

Right bottom, a photograph of the Wilhelm Gustloff after she was completed (Steamship Historical Society/University of Baltimore Library).

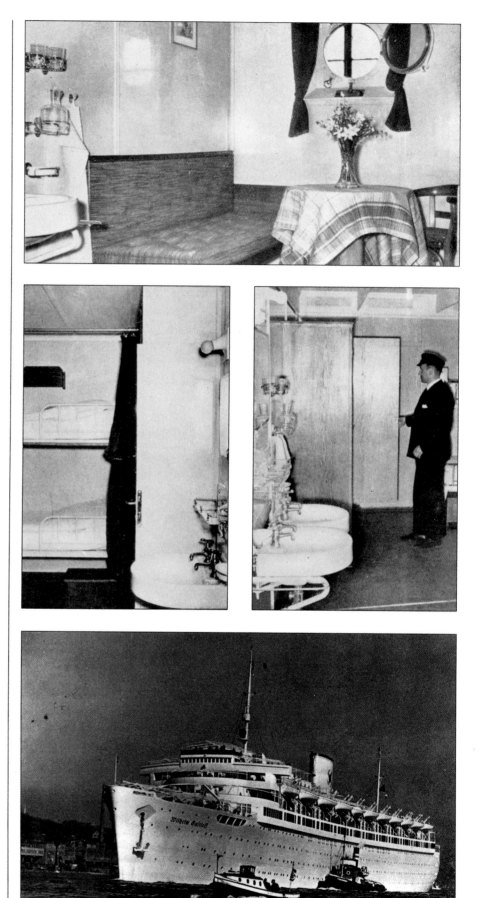

Ocean Liners Lost During the War: Part One, The Italians

The Italians suffered enormous tonnage losses during the course of the war. The two flagships of the Italian merchant marine, the 51,000 ton *Rex*, the Blue Ribband holder and the largest liner ever built in Italy, was sunk by Allied bombs on September 9, 1944. The slightly smaller running mate of the *Rex*, the 48,500 ton *Conte Di Savoia*, had suffered a similar fate on September 11,1943. Neither vessel was actively engaged in military work. Both were scrapped after the war.

The Italian Line endured two other major losses in the closing days of the war that were lesser only in comparison with the *Rex* and *Conte Di Savoia*. The 30,400 ton *Augustus* was sunk by the Germans in September, 1944, and the 32,500 ton *Roma* was sunk by Italian partisons on April 19, 1945. In addition to all of the above, the 24,200 *Duilio* was sunk in July, 1944, the 21,600 ton *Giulio Cesare* went down in September, 1944, and the 12,000 ton *Colombo* had been sunk in April, 1941.

The affiliated Lloyd Sabaudo Line also suffered heavy tonnage losses. The 17,000 ton *Conte*

New 54,000 ton "REX" of the *Italian Line*
De Luxe Speed King of the Southern Route
Maiden Voyage from New York October 8. 1932

Rosso was sunk in May, 1941, and the 18,700 ton *Conte Verde* was sunk in December, 1944.

The fact that most of these shipwrecks involved no serious loss of life was encouraging. Still, it was small compensation for the virtual decimation of the Italian passenger fleet.

Below, an Italian Line illustration of the Rex at the time of her maiden voyage. One wonders how they were measuring tonnage; all other sources list the Rex at just over 51,000 tons.

Top, the Conte Di Savoia.
Center, the Roma.

Ocean Liners Lost During the War: Part Two, The Germans

The German merchant marine was all but wiped out by the war. The Hamburg America Line and North German Lloyd between them lost at least ten major ships. Only the *Europa* among major liners survived to carry the German flag into the postwar era--and it was turned over to the French Line as war reparations. Then, in the process of being fitted out as the *Liberte*, she drifted into the wreck of the *Paris* at Le Havre and sank! (She was, it should be noted, later refloated.) The war was tough on the German passenger liner fleet.

Hamburg America Line losses included four Ballin-Class ships,

St. Louis were also lost during the course of the war.

North German Lloyd losses were equally severe. The *Bremen* was set afire by a disgruntled cabin boy in March, 1942, and totally destroyed. The 32,300 ton *Columbus* (sister ship to White Star's *Homeric*) was scuttled by her crew in December, 1939, in order to keep her from falling into British hands. The 14,600 ton *General von Steuben* and the

15,200 ton *Berlin* were sunk near the end of the war. The *Berlin* was raised by the Soviets and rebuilt as the *Admiral Nakhimov*, which sank again in 1986. Twice was the charm, though; the old *Berlin* is gone for good.

Left, the Europa (Steamship Historical Society/University of Baltimore Library).
Below, the New York and the Columbus.

Hansa, Deutschland, Hamburg and *New York*, that were lost in the last days of the war while assisting in the evacuation of the eastern territories. These were 21,000-22,000 ton liners that served as second echelon vessels alongside NGL's Bremen and Europa. The *Deutschland* alone evacuated 70,000 persons in seven trips before being sunk. The 19,500 ton *Resolute* and the 16,700 ton

Ocean Liners Lost During the War: Part Three, The Canadians

The 42,300 ton *Empress of Britain* was the largest liner ever to enter the Canadian service for Canadian Pacific or for any other line. She was considered by many to be among the most lovely ships afloat, possessing that perfection of proportion that was a hallmark of CPR design. She was launched on June 11, 1930, and entered service on May 27, 1931.

The *Empress of Britain* began serving as a troop transport in November, 1939. On October 26, 1940, while en route from Canada to Britain, she was attacked by a German bomber some 70 miles off the northwest coast of Ireland. Forty-nine persons died. The Polish destroyer, *Burza*, took the *Empress* in tow but two days later a German submarine, *U-32*,

finished her off with two torpedoes.

The 20,000 ton *Duchess of Athol* and her sister, the *Duchess of York*, were similarly sunk during trooping duties with a total of 15 lives lost. The 16,400 ton *Montrose* was sunk by a German torpedo on December 2, 1940, while serving as an armed merchant cruiser.

The *Empress of Canada* was sunk by an Italian submarine in the South Atlantic in 1943. There were 392 listed among the dead. In 1942, the *Empress of Asia* was bombed by the Japanese at Singapore with 19 dead.

Below, the Empress of Britain crossing the Panama Canal.

Right, top to bottom, the Empress of Canada, the Duchess of York, the Empress of Asia and the Empress of Russia, which made it through the war in one piece then caught fire while being reconverted to peacetime condition after the war.

Ocean Liners Lost During the War:
Part Four, The British

The Cunard Line, then officialy Cunard White Star, suffered several significant losses during World War II, including one of the three most serious losses of life in shipping history: the *Lancastria*, which is covered here in another section. Anywhere from 3,000-5,000 persons died when the *Lancastria* went down, depending the report you believe.

The sinking of the *Laconia* was less devastating in terms of loss of life, but contained aspects that made it unique in the anals of the war. The *Laconia* was a 19,600 ton liner that had been built in 1922 for the North Atlantic service but was often used for cruising during the 1930s. In April, 1942, the *Laconia* was transporting Italian prisoners of war when she was torpedoed by German submarine *U-156*. A total of 2,732 people were on board, including 1,800 Italian prisoners.

Upon approaching the scene of the sinking, the U-Boat commander realised who was on board and commenced a rescue operation. Soon vessels from the Italian Navy and the Vichy French Government were on the scene. At one point, the *U-156* herself had 260 survivors on board. The *U-156*, collected the *Laconia's* lifeboats together, raised a Red Cross flag and solicited Allied assistance on open radio frequencies. The result was a bomb attack from an American "Liberator" bomber. Another German submarine participating in the rescue, the *U-506*, was similarly attacked the following day. In response to this, the German Navy ordered its submarines to call off the rescue in this instance and to cease rescuing survivors of sunken ships in the future. Vichy French vessels were, however, able to take 1,111

survivors on board. Astonishingly, the British raised the breaking off of the rescue at Nuremberg as an example of German atrocities.

The two greatest potential disasters to Cunard ships left the vessels involved more or less unscathed--but not by much. Both *Queens* were fitted out as troop carriers and did incredible work transporting American, Australian and Canadian troops to the European front. Churchill credited

Above, for a few days in 1940 the three largest ocean liners ever built were docked together in New York. From left to right, the Normandie, the Queen Mary and the Queen Elizabeth.

Opposite, this is the last sight seen by crewmen on the H.M.S. Curacao (Steamship Historical Society/University of Baltimore Library).

them with shortening the war by at least a year. Each ship was capable of carrying at one time as many as 15,000 soldiers! This made any potential calamity involving them all the more staggering.

In February, 1944, the *Queen Elizabeth* came terrifyingly close to capsizing in a bad storm off the northern coast of Ireland. She was rolling heavily and suddenly took a severe list to port, at which point her quartermaster reported to the captain that she was out of control. She then took a further lurch to port, attaining a list of 37°! The sky was visible out the starboard side of the wheelhouse, while all one could see to port was sea and several more degrees would have sent her over for sure. The captain quickly ordered the quartermaster to release the wheel and--painfully slowly--she regained her footing and returned to vertical. It had been close, indeed.

The *Queen Mary* was involved in a serious collision during the war, an event that was hushed up at the time but which has become a favorite "war story" among modern-day ocean liner buffs. On October 2, 1942, while transporting 15,000 American troops off the northern coast of Ireland, the *Queen Mary* was being escorted by an aging British destroyer, the 4,200 ton *Curacao*, and six other warships. All were engaged in zig-zag patterns to confuse German submarines known to patrol the area. Gradually the *Mary* began to overtake the slower *Curacao*. Then, suddenly, the destroyed zigged when she should have zagged and found herself crossing directly in front of the onrushing *Queen*! It was all over in seconds. The *Queen Mary* sliced straight through the destroyer, like a knife through soft butter. Of 439 officers and men on board the *Curacao*, 338 perished. Nor could the liner stop to render assistance. She did not dare for she was under strict military orders not to stop for any

reason. So, it was left to the other ships in the escort to rescue what survivors they could find. The damage to the *Queen Mary* was serious. Her stem was badly buckled and she was taking water through an eleven foot gash. She limped into Scotland for a temporary patch and was then sent to Boston for permanent repairs. The story was not released to the public until 1945.

The White Star end of Cunard White Star suffered losses as well,

Below, the Georgic decked out as a troopship in 1945.
Right, the Queen Elizabeth on trooping duties during the war.

Above top, the old Pittsburgh, formerly of the White Star Line. Launched in 1920, she was transferred to the British-owned Red Star Line in 1925 and renamed the Pennland, later, sold to the Holland-America Line. She was bombed out and sunk in the Gulf of Athens in 1941.

Above bottom, the Carinthia. Along with the Laconia, she was of the Sythia-Class built for Cunard. In June, 1940, she was sunk by a German submarine, U-46, off the Irish coast. Although she remained afloat for 30 hours, she eventually slipped beneath the sea. Four persons died.

Right, did you ever wonder what really happens when a ship is struck by a torpedo? There aren't many ships that survive for show and tell, but this unnamed steamer did. She probably survived because the torpedo hit so far astern (Steamship Historical Society/University of Baltimore Library).

although the roster of White Star ships had been drastically depleted since the merger of the two lines in 1934. It was determined at that time that, considering the economic depression, the combined company simply had too many ships. Unfortunately, the solution for this seems to have been to get rid of the White Star fleet. Those ships that could not be sold were scrapped until only the *Georgic* and *Britannic*, among major White Star liners, remained. The *Britannic* got through the war in good shape, but the *Georgic* was bombed off Port Tewfik, Egypt, on July 14, 1941,

Left top, the Laconia.
Left center, the Runic torpedoed off Galway in 1940.
Left bottom, the Suevic, sister White Star liner to the Runic (see pages 35-39). She had been sold off and was scuttled by her Norwegian crew in 1942 to keep her from falling to the Germans.

burned and was beached in shallow water. She was deemed to be unsalvageable but wartime tonnage needs were so severe that an effort was made anyway. The result was the refloating and refitting of the *Georgic*, a monumental task that was not completed until December, 1944!

The loss of the *Ceramic* is covered elsewhere in this book. By the war, the *Ceramic* was no longer owned by Cunard White Star, but she had been White Star's flagship in the Australian service for many years, was highly regarded and was a particularly lovely ship, to boot. White Star enthusiasts--and there are many to this day--cannot regard the *Ceramic* as anything but a White Star ship.

Other Cunard ship losses included the 13,900 ton *Andania* and the 20,200 ton *Carinthia*. Despite these losses, Cunard came out of the war in better shape than many passenger lines.

Right top, the 12,800 ton Andorra Star, of the Blue Star Line. In May, 1940, she was transporting 1,178 German and Italian prisoners and 430 Allied personnel when she was torpedoed off Ireland. Panic on board made it difficult to abandon ship and there were 761 deaths: 148 Allied; 143 German and 470 Italian.

Right center, the Anchor Line's 16,900 ton Transylvania. In 1940, she was torpedoed and sank with 48 dead.

Right bottom, the Caledonia, the Transylvania's sister, was also torpedoed in 1940. Six died when she went down.

151

Chapter Six
SHIPWRECKS, 1950-1959

The 1950s continued the relatively quiet times enjoyed by commercial passenger service in the 1940s. In fact, there were only 10 notable shipwrecks during the whole decade. Among these, there were only two significant losses of life at sea and the total lives lost were only 161, making this the second safest decade to date for commercial passenger shipping.

The first shipwreck involved the 11,000 ton *Maipu*, of Cia Argentina de Navigacion Dodero. On November 4, 1951, she was wrecked near Weser Lightship. There were no fatalities.

On December 22,1952, the *Champollion*, a 12,000 ton Messageries Maritimes liner, was wrecked off Beirut in bad weather. The bridge crew had been confused by an airport beacon and ran the ship onto a reef. The terrified passengers were trapped on board by the weather as the ship slowly cracked in two and 15 passengers died trying to swim for shore. Eventually, small craft were able to rescue all of the remaining persons on board.

The year 1953 saw two wrecks, neither of them costing lives. On January 8th, the 10,000 ton *Klipfontein*, of United Netherlands Navigation, was wrecked off Cape Barra. Then, on January 25th, the 20,000 ton *Empress of Canada* (ex-*Duchess of Richmond*), of the Canadian Pacific line, burned while undergoing repairs in the Gladstone Drydock and was declared a total loss.

There were no shipwrecks at all involving regularly scheduled liners in either 1954 or 1955. The luck ran out in 1956, though. In that year, there were only two shipwrecks--and one of them, the 6,400 ton *Altair*, of the Rotterdam South America Line wrecked off Brazil, did not amount to much-- but the other was significant, indeed: the *Andrea Doria*.

The Italian Line had been virtually wiped out by the

vissitudes of war and the 29,000 ton *Doria* (together with her sister, the *Cristoforo Colombo*) was the opening salvo in Italy's effort to reclaim its position on the North Atlantic. That effort suffered a serious blow when, on July 25, 1956, the *Andrea Doria* collided off Nantucket with the Swedish liner, *Stockholm*. The *Doria* sank within hours and 51 persons died.

The next two years were relatively peaceful. The only major loss was the Greek Line's 10,000 ton liner, *Neptunia*, which was wrecked off Cobh on November 2, 1957. There were no lives lost.

Opposite, the Express of Canada that burned in 1953.

Above, the Skubryn afire in the Indian Ocean (Steamship Historical Society/University of Baltimore Library).

Right, the Neptunia.

The following year, on March 31st, the 9,700 ton *Skubryn*, of I. M. Skaugen, burned in the Indian Ocean. Again, no lives were lost.

Most Americans are only vaguely aware--if at all--that Greenland is a Danish possession. The Danes, however, are proud of the fact and determined to maintain all possible links between the two distantly removed parts of the

globe. To that end, the 2,800 ton *Hans Hedtoft*, with an ice-breaker bow, was launched in 1958 for the purpose of maintaining a year-round sea link with Greenland. On January 30, 1959, on the return leg of its maiden voyage, it apparently struck an iceberg and was lost with all hands. A total of 95 persons perished in this, the last significant shipwreck of the 1950s.

ITALIAN LINE

G. Colombo / A. D

The Perils of Over-Confidence: The Sinking of the Andrea Doria

The Italian passenger ship fleet had been virtually wiped out during World War II. When, after the war, the Italian Line sought to re-establish its position on the North Atlantic, it set about building two new ships, 29,000 tonners, that came to be known as the *Andrea Doria* and the *Cristoforo*

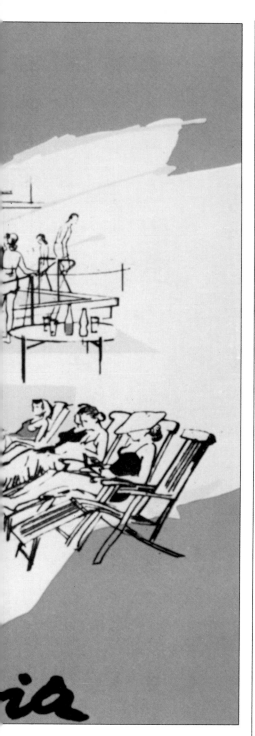

Colombo. The *Doria* came first. She was launched in 1951 and entered service on January 14, 1953. The *Colombo* followed 18 months later.

The *Doria* and the *Colombo* were not identical twins. Although they were virtually indistinguishable from the outside, they differed to a considerable degree in their interior appointments. The *Doria* was the flagship of the line and, frankly, she got special treatment. Only the finest quality furnishings, artworks and materials were used in her and she quickly assumed a position of prominence in the Genoa-New York service.

On July 25, 1956, the *Andrea Doria* and the Swedish America liner, *Stockholm*, collided off Nantucket Island in the fog. The *Stockholm* rammed the starboard

Above, the original Italian Line Andrea Doria/Colombo brochure. Right, the Cristoforo Colombo, the Doria's sister. Right bottom, the Stockholm. Following Pages, the sinking of the Andrea Doria (Steamship Historical Society/University of Baltimore Library).

side of the *Doria* making a huge gash well into the Italian ship and well below the waterline.

In its outlines, the collision was very reminiscent of the *Empress of Ireland* disaster of 1914. Fortunately, there was dramatically less carnage. Only 51 people died from both ships, mostly on the *Doria*. The death toll was reduced by the fact that the *Doria* remained afloat for some 12 hours, compared to the estimated 14 <u>minutes</u> of the *Empress of Ireland*. Help was soon to arrive,

as well. The *Stockholm* boarded some of the *Doria's* passengers, while the French Line's *Ile de France* took most of the rest.

Following contentious hearings and litigation, the bridge crews of both liners were faulted and both lines agreed to assume the burden of their own losses. That meant, as a practical matter, that the Italian Line was accepting major responsibility for the wreck since its damages far exceeded those of the Swedish America Line.

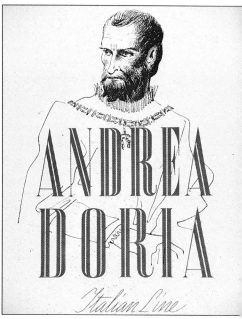

On these and the following pages are photographs of life on board the Andrea Doria. Opposite, this wonderful shot was probably taken from the port wing bridge. Top center, a cabin class three-berth stateroom. Bottom center, an example of the caloric intake awaiting Doria passengers. Left, a passenger relaxing in a first class stateroom. Below, fun in the sun at the Doria's cabin class swimming pool. Following pages, the ornate first class ballroom, one of the Doria's finest public rooms.

162

Chapter Seven
SHIPWRECKS, 1960-1969

The 1940s and 1950s had been relatively quiet in the passenger trade. In the 1960s, the situation heated up once again. There were 20 notable shipwrecks between 1960 and 1969 and fully 15 of them involved fire. Much of this was due to the rise of the cruise lines, most of which bought up older ships from established lines and registered them in Panama or Liberia. In an increasing number of cases, these ships were subject to breakdowns of various kinds-- mechanical, electrical and so forth-- and fires were the all too frequent result. Complicating matters, ship owners increasingly tried to make do with cheaper, but sometimes inexperienced, crews to man their vessels, thus by-passing the well-organized and demanding European and American maritime unions. Often, the tragic result of this type of economizing was that when a *Lakonia* or a *Yarmouth Castle* caught fire at sea, few crewmen knew what to do.

The first serious wreck involved the 8,400 ton *Alcoa Corsair*, of the Alcoa Steamship Company. On October 22, 1960, she was in a collision in the Mississippi River that cost 10 lives. On December 14th, the *Tarsus*, a 9,400 ton liner of the Turkish Maritime Lines, burned in the Bosphorus. No lives were lost in that incident, but a much more serious one was soon to follow.

On April 7, 1961, the *Dara*, a 5,000 ton liner of the British India Steam Navigation Company, burned at Dubai with a loss of 238 lives out of a reported 819 on board. On July 8th, of that same year, the 2,000 Portugese colonial steamer *Save*, of the Compania Colonial de Navegacao, burned off Mozambique. Of 549 persons on board, a reported 259 perished. Still later that year, on October 22nd, the 18,000 ton *Bianca C*, of the Costa Armatori Line, burned at Granada with a loss of four lives.

On March 14, 1962, the 18,000 ton *Venezuela (ex-De Grasse, ex-Empress of Australia)*, then owned by the Sicuia Oceanica Societa per Azioni, was wrecked off Cannes without loss of life.

The next important shipwreck did not transpire until April 8, 1963, when the 16,000 ton *Brittany (ex-Bretagne)*, of the Chandris Lines, burned in Greece while undergoing engine repairs. There were no deaths.

The world's attention was riveted to the Atlantic Ocean in December, 1963, when the *Lakonia (ex-Johan van Oldenbarnevelt)*, a 20,000 ton Greek Line ship, burned off of the Canary Islands with a loss of 89 lives accounted for, 42 more missing. The ineptitude of the crew played a big role in the loss of life.

The following year, 1964, was quiet until November 19th, when the 11,000 ton *Rio de la Plata*, of Flota Mercante del Estado, burned at Buenos Aires. Fortunately, there were no lives lost.

The same could not be said for the next major shipwreck, that of the *Yarmouth Castle*. The *Yarmouth Castle* started life as the *Evangeline*, a 5,000 ton coastal steamer plying the waters between Boston and the Caribbean. Launched in 1927, the *Yarmouth Castle* was virtually an antique when she began sailing for the Yarmouth Cruise Lines in the 1960s. On November 13, 1965, she caught fire en route from Miami to the Bahamas with the loss of 87 lives.

In April, 1966, the *Viking Princess (ex-Lavoisier)*, a 12,000 ton ship sailed by A/S Berge Sigval Bergesen, burned off Guantanamo Bay, Cuba. None died. Later that year, on September 7th, the *Hanseatic (ex-Empress of Japan, ex-Empres of Scotland)*, a 30,000 ton ship

operated by the Hamburg-Atlantic Line, burned at Port Everglades. There were no fatalities but the ship was a total loss.

Still another ship saw the last of her days that year, on December 12th, although not by fire. The *Heraklion* (ex-*Leicestershire*), an 8,900 ton Typaldos Lines ship, was sunk in bad weather off Greece through the incompetence of her crew. They had failed to batten-down the cargo and a truck below decks broke through two of the forward freight doors, thus letting in the water that swamped the ship. A total of 241 persons drowned as a result.

The following year, 1968, was an unusually active one for shipwrecks. On March 20, 1968, the 10,000 ton *Elisabethville*, of the Compagnie Maritime Belge, burned at Antwerp with no loss of life. On April 11th of that same year, the 8,900 ton ocean-going car ferry *Wahine*, of the Union Steamship Co. of New Zealand, was wrecked in hurricane force winds off Wellington with the loss of 51 lives. Remarkably, 699 persons survived. On April 17th, the *Rio Jachal*, an 11,000 ton ship

Above, the Johan van Oldenbarnevelt which later in life became the Lakonia.

Below, the Venezuela, ex-De Grasse, ex-Empress of Australia (Steamship Historical Society/ University of Baltimore Library).

operated by Flota Mercante del Estado, burned at Buenos Aires. There were no casualties. On May 21st, the 4,700 ton *Blenheim*, of the Fred Olsen Company, burned in the North Sea. Again, there were no casualties.

There were only two wrecks in 1969, and no deaths. In January, the *Fairsea*, a 13,000 ton Alvion liner, burned off Balboa. On August 12th, the *Paraguay Star*, a 10,000 ton Blue Star liner, burned at London.

A Cruise to Nowhere:
The Final Voyage of the Yarmouth Castle

The *Yarmouth Castle* started life as the *Evangeline*. Built in 1927 in the Cramp yards in Philadelphia, and designed to carry 350 passengers in one class, the 5,000 ton *Evangeline* served as a cruise ship out of Boston to Yarmouth in the summer and out of New York to the Caribbean in the winter. Except for a stint in government service during World War II, this was the life of the *Evangeline* until 1954. In that year, she was switched to Liberian registry and began cruise service out of Miami.

In 1963, the *Evangeline* was sold to Yarmouth Cruises and renamed the *Yarmouth Castle*. The intention was to service the Caribbean out of New York, but the elderly ship was not up to the task. Charges and counter charges flew between the Caribbean Cruise Line, which managed the ship, and the ships owners, while customers were stranded in New York. Finally, the *Yarmouth Castle* was placed on the shorter Miami-to-Nassau run.

During the night of November 13, 1965, the *Yarmouth Castle* met her end in what came to be regarded as the most important liner mishap in American waters since the *Andrea Doria*. Under the command of a Greek captain, Byron Voutsinas, and a scratch crew of 174, the *Yarmouth Castle* was on the way to Nassau with 371 passengers. Just after midnight, fire broke out in a storage room and quickly spread through out much of the ship. The crew tried to fight the conflagration but did not inform the captain for nearly half-an-hour, at which time he did not order an SOS or take

any obvious action to alert his passengers. Within minutes, the bridge was engulfed in flame and no radio messages could be sent.

The cruise liner, *Bahama Star*, and the freighter, *Finnpulp*, saw the glow in the nighttime sky and raced to investigate. The first lifeboat that got off from the *Yarmouth Castle* included, among others, Captain Voutsinas and two of his senior officers. The captain of the *Finnpulp*, was so incensed at this behavior he ordered the officers of the *Yarmouth Castle* to return to their ship and assist in the evacuation. In the end, 458 persons were rescued, leaving a death toll of only 87, which could have been far worse considering the circumstances. Shortly after 6:00 am, the *Yarmouth Castle* capsized and sank.

The *Yarmouth Castle* wreck prompted a re-examination in the United States of shipping regulations and standards as they applied to cruise liners of foreign registry. This has resulted in a significant improvement of safety standards to the benefit of all who sail with the increasingly popular cruise lines.

Left, the Evangeline while in military service during World War II and looking a bit the worse for wear. She was then nearly 20 years old (Steamship Historical Society/University of Baltimore).

The Evengeline was kicked around from owner to owner in her last years. She began life as a hurricane decker for service out of Boston and New York and ended up in cruise service out of Miami under Liberian registry. By that point, her engines were old and troublesome and all the problems that befall aging ships were beginning to develop. The two photos, above, show her in her later years, alone and with her sister. The card, bottom, was sent by a passenger in July, 1965. The message read: "Having a great time on this wonderful ship!"

167

Chapter Eight
SHIPWRECKS, 1970-1979

The decade of the 1970s continued the trend toward trouble involving superannuated ships handed down to cruise lines with Greek, Panamanian or Liberian registries. The burning of the *Lakonia* and the *Yarmouth Castle*, however, had sparked a new look at government regulations. This was particularly true of the burgeoning cruise industry, an industry that had not been given much special attention heretofore. With the traditional transatlantic passenger routes all but put out of business by the jet airplane, cruise service had now become the bulk of the business.

Although there were a score of shipwrecks during this, the eighth decade of the century, there were only 126 lives lost and most of them were on one ship. Seventeen of the 20 shipwrecks in the 1970s involved no loss of life at all. Evidently, all the years of ever tightening safety standards and regulations were paying off.

In 1970, there was only one shipwreck of note. On July 20th the *Fulvia*, a 16,000 ton Costa Armatoria liner, burned off Canary Islands. No deaths were reported.

The following year saw three significant shipwrecks. On January 8th, the *Antilles*, a 19,000 ton CGT ship, caught fire and burned, off Mustique in the Caribbean, continuing a decades-long battle the French Line had had with fire. Fortunately, there were no fatalities, although the ship sank the next day. A total of 690 people were rescued by, among others, the *QE2*. The *Antilles* was the last French Line ship built expressly for Caribbean service.

Later in the year, on August 28th, the *Helcanna*, an 11,000 ton Greek ship owned by the C. S. Efthymiadis Line, burned near Brindisi. Of an estimated 1,000 persons on board, only 24 died, but Italian authorities arrested the captain for multiple homicide for carrying too many passengers, having inadequate fire-fighting equipment and failure to deal in a competent way with the crisis. Finally, in 1971, on September

Left, the Angelina Lauro (Steamship Historical Society/ University of Baltimore Library).

168

8th, the 10,000 ton *Monte Udala*, of the Naviera Aznar Line, while in the Italian-South American service, sprung a leak and sank off Ilheus. There were, however, no fatalities.

The next year, 1972, saw the greatest passenger ship catastrophe of all-time, at least insofar as the size of the ship was concerned, when the *Queen Elizabeth* was destroyed by fire in Hong Kong. Two other small liners burned that year, the 6,000 ton *Marmara* of the Turkish Maritime Lines and the 8,200 ton *Oriental Warrior* (ex-*Hamburg*) of the United Overseas Export Line. On September 23, 1972, the *Caribia* (ex-*Vulcania*), a 24,496 ton liner, was wrecked on the rocks at Cannes. Sabotage was suggested, but no one died. The ship, however, was a total loss.

The year 1973 saw three more burnings of passenger liners. The 10,800 ton *Knossoss*, of the C. S. Efthymiadis Line, burned off Greece, and the *Satrustegui*, 6,600 ton ship operated by Transatlantica Espanola, burned at Barcelona. On July 1st, the *Homeric* (formerly the *Mariposa*) an 18,563 ton cruise liner operated by the Home Lines, burned off New York. There were no deaths but the ship was lost.

Fire raged again in 1974. The 11,700 ton *Malaysia Kita*, of the Fir Line, burned at Singapore, and the 14,000 ton *Cunard Ambassador* burned off Key West. There were no lives lost in either shipwreck and the *Cunard Ambassador* was returned to

Right, the Caribia, ex-Coronia (Steamship Historical Society/ University of Baltimore Library).

service, although not by Cunard. The year also saw the demise of another old Cunarder, the *Caribia*.

The *Caribia* had started out as the 34,000 ton *Coronia*, of the Cunard Line. Designed as a first class-only liner, the *Coronia* had an uneventful career until she was put to pasture in the mid-1960s. After that she was renamed and knocked around for a while looking for backers until, in 1974, she was sold to the breakers in Taiwan. En route to Taiwan, the *Caribia*, under tow, was wrecked on August 13th on the breakwater at Guam. She was subsequently broken up on the spot.

Following the wreck of the *Caribia*, everything else in the 1970s that came to grief burned. In 1976, the 12,100 ton *Belle Abeto* (ex-*Laennec*), of the Compania de Navigation Abeto, burned at Sasebo, the 11,700 ton *Malaysia Raya* (ex-*Laos*), of the Fir Line,

burned at Port Kelang, the 11,300 ton *Blue Sea* (ex-*Europa*), of Ahmed Mohammed Baahoud, burned at Jeddah, the 3,800 ton *Mecca* (ex-*Gullfoss*), of Orri Navigation Lines burned, also at Jeddah, and the 3,900 ton *Patra* (ex-*Kronprins Frederik*), then owned by Arab Navigators, burned off Saudi Arabia. The only incident involving loss of life was the *Patra*, where an estimated 100 persons died in the December 25th fire.

The following year saw only one shipwreck. On June 2, 1977, the 18,700 ton *Rasa Sayang* (ex-*Bergensfjord*), then operated by Michaelis Strouhakis, burned in the Strait of Malacca with two deaths. That was the last major wreck of the decade save one: On March 30, 1979, the 24,300 ton *Angelina* (ex-*Oranje*), of the Achille Lauro Line, burned at St. Thomas. There were no lives lost, but the ship was totalled.

The Death of a Queen:
The Burning of the Seawise University

Few recognize the name *"Seawise University,"* but she was the largest passenger liner ever sunk. In fact, she was the largest passenger liner ever built, although not under that odd name. The *Seawise University* was, in fact, the *Queen Elizabeth*.

The 83,673 ton *Queen Elizabeth* had been launched in March, 1940, as a running mate for the *Queen Mary*. She was intended to carry 2,283 passengers in three classes. The launching did not take place, however, until after the outbreak of World War II and the unfinished ship was sent to the United States for fitting out. This was done as a troop carrier, not as

a passenger liner. In that guise the *Elizabeth* steamed half-a-million miles on trooping duties, carrying some 800,000 men. After the war, she was returned to Cunard and finally fitted out for passenger service, which she commenced in the latter months of 1946.

From that point on, the career of the *Queen Elizabeth* was remarkable only for its success. The *Elizabeth* and the *Mary* maintained weekly service between New York and Southampton for many years until the advent of the jet age finally did them in. The *Elizabeth* was taken out of service in October, 1968, after 22 years of successful sailing on the North

Atlantic run.

Initially, the idea was to turn her into a tourist attraction in

Above, the Queen Elizabeth as depicted in a 1960s Cunard publicity photograph.

Opposite, the Seawise University, ex-Queen Elizabeth. Although completely refurbished, the Seawise University was largely unaltered in terms of its interior decor. The Seawise University was conceived as a one-class, first class-only ship. The "university" part of the show was not an immediate prospect. At first it was intended to be a high class cruise liner in the Pacific.

Announcing the Maiden Voyage of SEAWISE (formerly the R.M.S. Queen Elizabeth) 75-day Circle Pacific Cruise.

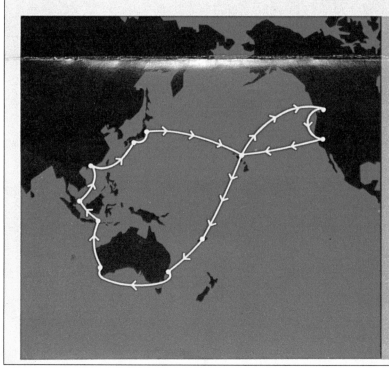

Sailing from Los Angeles on April 24, 1972. Rates from $30 a day first class.

Sailing from Vancouver, B.C. on April 18, 1972

	ARRIVAL DATE	DEPARTURE DATE
Los Angeles		April 24 PM
Honolulu	April 29 AM	May 3 AM
Suva	May 10 AM	May 12 PM
Sydney	May 16 AM	May 18 PM
Fremantle	May 23 AM	May 25 AM
Bali	May 28 noon	May 31 AM
Singapore	June 2 AM	June 5 AM
Hong Kong	June 8 AM	June 11 AM
Kobe	June 14 noon	June 16 PM
Yokohama	June 17 AM	June 20 PM
Honolulu	June 26 noon	June 29 AM
Vancouver	July 4 noon	July 6 PM
Los Angeles	July 9 AM	

Ports of call and dates subject to change without notice.

Florida, much as was done with the *Queen Mary* in Long Beach, California. These plans fell through, however, for financial and other reasons and the *Elizabeth* was sold to C. Y. Tung, a Hong Kong shipping magnate, who announced plans to turn her into a floating university and cruise liner. She was accordingly sent to Hong Kong for an extensive refit, arriving in July, 1971, and emerging nearly completed by the end of the year as the *Seawise University*.

On the morning of January 9, 1972, the *Seawise University* erupted in flames. Fire seemed to come from everywhere all at once and arson was almost certainly the cause. Fireboats were quickly called in and battled the blaze for hours before finally giving up. The following day the *Seawise University* (ex-*Queen Elizabeth*), the largest liner ever built, rolled over onto her starboard side in

shallow water. No attempt to refloat her was ever made and she was broken up on the spot beginning in 1974.

On these pages, the tragic end of the Seawise University. The fire broke out on January 9, 1972. On January 10th, the ship capsized and was given up as a total loss, but it was not until January 13th that the fire finally died out. The Seawise University had a troubled career from the very beginning, counting the three years she spent languishing in financial trouble in Port Everglades, Florida, being kicked around from owner to owner. On February 10, 1971, after suffering the humiliation of being sold at auction, she left Florida for Hong Kong. She experienced serious boiler trouble on the trip and was held up several times en route as a consequence (Steamship Historical Society/ University of Baltimore Library).

Chapter Nine
SHIPWRECKS, 1980-1986

The decade of the 1980s, which is not over as this is written, has been characterized by a variety of disasters. There have been the usual third world conflagrations. There have been the usual older passenger liners that have fallen into new hands coming to grief in one way or another in parts of the world they were never meant to sail. And, there have been new ships built for cruising that have suffered calamitous mishaps. There has been, in short, a lot more variety than in the 1970s when nearly everything burned and that was that.

On March 3, 1980, the first wreck occurred when the *Leonardo Da Vinci*, the 33,300 ton former flagship of the Italian Line, burned at La Spezia. The ship was destroyed but there was no loss of life. In April, the 7,200 ton *Ernesto Anastasio*, of Compania Transmediterranea, was wrecked off Spain, again without loss of life. In August, the 18,700 ton *Rasa Sayang* (ex-*Bergensfjord*) burned--for the second and last time--at Perama, and, on October 4th, the *Prinsendam*, an 8,500 ton cruise ship of the Holland America Cruises, burned in Gulf of Alaska. No one died, but it was a spectacular fire, with the rescue operation carried out by the Coast Guard and the *Williamsburg*, a supertanker. The passengers and crew were gotten off within hours. On October 11th, with the fire still raging in the bowels of the ship, the *Prinsendam* rolled over and sank 79 miles west of Sitka.

There were three shipwrecks in 1981. The 13,500 ton *Reina Del Mar* (ex-*Ocean Monarch*), burned at Perama, the 4,400 ton *Syria*, of the Egyptian Navigation Company, was wrecked off Crete, and the 6,400 ton *Arion*, of the Maritime Company of Lesvos, burned at Haifa. There were no losses of life.

There were two shipwrecks in 1982. The 16,200 ton *Mediterranean Star* (ex-

Left, the always exquisite Leonardo da Vinci at Gibraltar.

МОРПАСФЛОТ
ВСЕСОЮЗНОЕ ОБЪЕДИНЕНИЕ МОРСКОГО
ПАССАЖИРСКОГО ФЛОТА

ул. Жданова ¹/₄
МОСКВА, К-12

Bloemfontein Castle), of the Karageogris Lines, burned in the Aegean and the 6,300 ton *Ciudad de Sevilla* (ex-*Infanta Beatrix*), of the Compaia Transmediterranea, was wrecked at Majorca. Again, there were no lives lost.

In 1983, the 4,500 ton *Atlantis* (ex-*Adonis*), of the K-Hellenic Lines, burned at Piraeus. Then, in 1984, the *Columbus C* (ex-*Kungsholm*), the 16,300 ton cruise liner of Costa Armatori, was wrecked at Cadiz. No one died in these shipwrecks, but, in 1985, 40 people died when the 17,200 ton *Chidambaram* (ex-*Pasteur*), then operated by the Shipping Corporation of India, burned off Madras.

The Soviets entered the fray

Above, the Soviet Cruise ship, Mikhail Lermontov.

Below, the Soviet's Admiral Nakhimov, ex-Berlin.

with a vengeance in 1986. On February 16th, their fourteen-year-old cruise liner *Mikhail Lermontov*, a 20,000 tonner with all the modern conveniences and operated by the Baltic Shipping Company, was wrecked in a storm off New Zealand. There was only one life lost--a crewman missing and presumed drowned--but 409 passengers and 229 crew survived.

Later in 1986, the 17,000 ton *Admiral Nakhimov*, formerly North German Lloyd's *Berlin*, and then operated by the Black Sea Shipping Company, was involved in a collision (errily reminiscent of the *Empress of Ireland* catastrophe) in the Black Sea with the Soviet bulk carrier, *Pyotr Vasev*. Of 888 passengers and 346 crewmen on board, 398 perished.

Appendix I

MAJOR PASSENGER LINER DISASTERS SINCE 1900

The shipwrecks contained in this section are limited to those passenger liners that were wrecked in peacetime or in wartime while engaged in scheduled passenger service. While no such compilation can purport to be absolutely complete, this listing comes as close as the publisher thought possible at the time this book went to press.

DATE	SHIP	TONS	BUILT	COMPANY	NATURE OF DISASTER	LOSS
Mar 9, 1900	Curvier	2,229	1883	Lamport & Holt	collision, Douvre	26
Apr 5, 1900	Mexican	4,661	1883	Union Steamship Co	collision, Wakefield	0
Jun 3, 1900	Devenum	2,298	1888	Andresen Line	wrecked, Oporto	n/a
Jun 30, 1900	Saale	4,967	1886	North German Lloyd	fire, Hoboken	99
Feb 22, 1901	City of Rio de Janeiro	3,548	1878	Pacific Mail Steamship Co	wrecked, off San Francisco	105
May 7, 1901	Tantallon Castle	5,636	1894	Union-Castle Line	wrecked, off Cape Town	0
Jun 26, 1901	Lusitania	3,912	1877	Elder Dempster	wrecked, near Cape Race	0
Jun 29, 1901	Armenia	3,396	1881	Anchor Line	wrecked, St. John	0
Jul 7, 1901	Mexico	2,101	1875	Spanish Trans-Atlantic Co	wrecked, off Portugal	0
Feb 9, 1902	Grecian	3,613	1880	Allan Line	wrecked, Halifax	n/a
Mar 5, 1902	Waesland	4,752	1867	American Line	collision, Harmonides	2
Mar 31, 1902	Lake Superior	4,562	1884	Elder Dempster	wrecked, near St. John	0
Apr, 1902	Camorta	2,119	1880	British India Steam Nav Co	storm, Gulf of Martaban	739
Sep 12, 1903	Bretagne	2,209	1877	SGTM	wrecked, off Bahia	0
May 6, 1904	Kurfurst	5,655	1901	Hamburg East-Africa Line	wrecked, off Portugal	0
Jun 28, 1904	Norge	3,310	1881	Scandanavian American Line	wrecked, off Rockall	est. 550
Jun 29, 1904	Australia	6,901	1892	P & O Line	wrecked, near Melbourne	0

Date	Ship	Tonnage	Year	Line	Fate	Deaths
Feb 7, 1905	Damara	1,779	1885	Furness, Withy & Co	foundered, off Musquodoboit	n/a
Feb 16, 1905	Orizaba	6,077	1886	Orient Line	wrecked, off Fremantle	0
Jun 23, 1905	Chodoc	4,686	1898	Chargeur Reunis	wrecked, near Gardafui	n/a
Jul, 1905	Rohilla Maru	3,869	1880	Toyo Kisen Kabushiki Kaisha	wrecked, China Inland Sea	n/a
Sep 5, 1905	Cyril	4,380	1883	Booth Line	collision, w/Anselm in Amazon	n/a
Nov 5, 1905	Bavarian	10,376	1899	Allan Line	wrecked, off Montreal	0
Jan 4, 1906	Caobang	6,762	1902	Messageries Maritimes	wrecked, off Poulo Condor	n/a
Jun 10, 1906	Etolia	3,270	1887	Elder Dempster	wrecked, near Cape Sable	0
Aug 4, 1906	Sirio	4,141	1883	Raggio Line	wrecked, off Hormigas Island	442
Nov 21, 1906	Kaiser Wilhelm der Gr.	14,349	1897	North German Lloyd	collision, off Cherbourg	5
Dec 16, 1906	Prinzessin Victoria Luise	4,409	1900	Hamburg American Line	wrecked, off Jamaica	1*

* The captain commited suicide.

Date	Ship	Tonnage	Year	Line	Fate	Deaths
Feb 24, 1907	Imperatrix	4,213	1888	Lloyd Austriaco	wrecked, off Crete	40
Mar 7, 1907	Dakota	20,714	1905	Great Northern Steam Ship Co	wrecked, near Yokohama	0
May 7, 1907	Poitou	2,679	1883	SGTM	wrecked, off Uruguay	20
Oct 17, 1907	Tartar	4,339	1883	Canadian Pacific	collision, off British Columbia	0
Oct 22, 1907	Borussia	6,951	1906	Hamburg American Line	foundered, at Lisbon	3
Mar 12, 1908	Newark Castle	6,224	1901	Union-Castle Line	wrecked, near Durban	3
May 10, 1908	Hohenzollern	6,661	1889	North German Lloyd	stranded, off Sardinia	0
Aug 3, 1908	Cap Frio	5,732	1900	Hamburg-South America Line	wrecked, off Brazil	n/a
Oct 16, 1908	Velasquez	7,542	1906	Lamport & Holt	stranded, near Santos, Brazil	0
Oct/Nov 1908	Neustria	2,926	1883	Fabre Line	disappeared, between NY-Marseille	n/a
Jan 23, 1909	Republic	15,378	1903	White Star Line	collision, off New York	4
Jun 10, 1909	Slavonia	10,606	1902	Cunard Line	wrecked, off Flores Island	0*
Jul, 1909	Waratah	9,339	1908	Blue Anchor Line	disappeared, off South Africa	92
Aug 4, 1909	Maori	5,200	1893	Shaw, Savill & Albion Co Ltd	wrecked, off Cape Town	34
Aug 5, 1909	Langton Grange	5,851	1896	Houlder Bros & Co Ltd	wrecked, off England	n/a
Aug 14, 1909	Lucania	12,952	1893	Cunard Line	burned, at Liverpool	0
Sep 6, 1909	Laurentian	3,983	1872	Allan Line	wrecked, off Tripassey Bay	0
Sep 15, 1909	Umhlali	3,388	1905	Natal Line	wrecked, near Cape Point	0
Nov 14, 1909	La Seyne	2,379	1873	Messageries Maritimes	collision, in Rheo Straits	101

Date	Ship	Tonnage	Year	Line	Disposition	Deaths
Feb 10, 1910	General Chanzy	2,257	1891	Cie Generale Transatlantique	wrecked, off Minorca	93
Mar 1, 1910	Korea	6,123	1899	Russian American Line	abandoned, North Atlantic	n/a
Mar 31, 1910	Pericles	10,925	1908	Aberdeen Line	wrecked, of Australia	0
Oct 23, 1910	Lisboa	7,412	1910	Empresa Nacional	wrecked, near Cape Town	7
Nov, 1910	Colombo	3,731	1882	Messageries Maritimes	damaged, Indochina	n/a
Dec 13, 1910	Delhi	8,080	1905	P & O Line	wrecked, off Morroco	0
Feb 13, 1911	New Guinea	2,674	1885	McIlwraith, McEacharn & Co	wrecked, off Australia	n/a
Apr 18, 1911	Lusitania	5,557	1906	Empresa Nacional	wrecked, on Bellows Rocks	4
Apr 22, 1911	Asia (ex-Doric)	4,744	1883	Pacific Mail Steamship Co	wrecked, off China	n/a
May 12, 1911	Merida	6,207	1906	NY & Cuba Mail Steamship Co	collision, off Cape Charles	0
Jun 15, 1911	Milton	2,679	1888	Lamport & Holt	wrecked, off Portugal	n/a
Jul 27, 1911	Empress of China	5,905	1891	Canadian Pacific	wrecked, off Yokohama	0
Sep 11, 1911	Papanui	6,582	1898	Australian Shipping Co	burned, off St. Helena	0
Jan 23, 1912	Claderon	4,083	1900	Lamport & Holt	collision, off Liverpool	0
Mar 16, 1912	Oceana	6,610	1888	P & O Line	collision, in English Channel	9
Apr 14, 1912	Titanic	46,238	1912	White Star Line	collision, in North Atlantic	1,503
Nov 6, 1912	Oravia	5,321	1897	Pacific Steam Navigation Co	wrecked, off Falkland Islands	n/a
Jan 16, 1913	Veronese	7,063	1906	Lamport & Holt	wrecked, off Portugal	43
Aug 25, 1913	Devon	5,489	1897	Federal Steam Navigation Co	wrecked, off Wellington	n/a
Oct 9, 1913	Volturno	3,581	1906	Uranium Steamship Co	burned, North Atlantic	136
Jan 13, 1914	Cobequid (ex-Goth)	4,791	1893	Royal Mail Lines	wrecked, off Newfoundland	n/a
May 29, 1914	Empress of Ireland	14,191	1905	Canadian Pacific	collision, in St. Lawrence	1,012
Oct 26, 1914	Vandyck	10,328	1911	Lamport & Holt	sunk by Germans, in S Atlantic	0
Nov 8, 1914	Norfolk	5,310	1900	Federal Steam Navigation Co	burned, off Australia	0
May 1, 1915	Lusitania	31,550	1907	Cunard Line	torpedoed, off Ireland	1,198
Aug, 1915	Marowijne	3,191	1908	United Fruit Co	disappeared, in Caribbean	n/a
Sep 19, 1915	Athinai	6,742	1908	Nat Steam Nav Co of Greece	burned, in North Atlantic	0
Oct 3, 1915	Highland Warrior	7,485	1911	Nelson Line	wrecked, off Spain	n/a
Nov 8, 1915	Ancona	8,885	1908	Italia Line	torpedoed, North Atlantic	194

Date	Ship	Tonnage	Year	Line	Cause, Location	Deaths
Jan 5, 1916	Thessaloniki	4,682	1889	Nat Steam Nav Co of Greece	storm, North Atlantic	0
Mar 3, 1916	Principe de Austurias	8,371	1914	Pinillos, Izquierdo y Compania	wrecked, off Brazil	415
Mar 31, 1916	Chiyo Maru	13,426	1908	Toyo Kisen KK	wrecked, off Hong Kong	0
Aug 30, 1916	Tongariro	7,661	1901	New Zealand Shipping	wrecked, off New Zealand	0
Dec 25, 1916	Maitai	3,393	1892	Union Steam Ship Co of NZ	wrecked, off Tonga	0
Jul 15, 1917	Kristianiafjord	10,669	1913	Norwegian America Line	wrecked, off Cape Race	0
Feb 5, 1918	Toscana	4,113	1900	Italia Societa di Nav a Vapore	collision, near Gibraltar	0
May 6, 1918	Highland Scot	7,604	1910	Nelson Line	wrecked, off Brazil	n/a
Sep 12, 1919	Valbanera	5,099	1906	Pinillos, Izquierdo y Compania	storm, off Cuba	488
Jan 20, 1920	Afrique	5,404	1907	Chargeur Reunis	wrecked, off Bay of Biscay	553
Mar 1, 1920	Bohemian	8,548	1900	Leyland Line	wrecked, off Nova Scotia	0
Mar 14, 1921	Grampion	10,187	1907	Allan Line	burned, at Antwerp	0
May 22, 1922	Egypt	7,912	1897	P & O Line	collision, off Egypt	86
May 31, 1922	Wiltshire	10,390	1912	Federal Steam Navigation Co	wrecked, off New Zealand	0
Oct 12, 1922	City of Honolulu (ex-Fiedrich der Grosse)	10,771	1896	Los Angeles Steamship Co	burned, off California	0
Nov, 1922	Monte Grappa	7,434	1921	Navigazione Libera Triestina	abandoned, North Atlantic	n/a
Apr 23, 1923	Mossamedes	4,615	1895	Empresa Nacional	abandoned, off Angola	31
May 21, 1923	Marvale(ex-Corsican)	11,439	1907	Canadian Pacific	wrecked, near Cape Race	0
Mar 17, 1926	Paporoa	6,563	1899	New Zealand Shipping	burned, South Atlantic	0
Jul 12, 1926	Fontainebleau	10,015	1924	Messageries Maritimes	burned, at Djibouti	0
Aug 24, 1926	Persia	6,283	1903	Lloyd Triestino	burned, off India	0
Nov 16, 1926	Braga	6,122	1907	Fabre Line	wrecked, off Greece	n/a
Oct 25, 1927	Principessa Mafalda	9,210	1909	Nav Gen Italiana Societa	explosion, off Brazil	303

181

Date	Ship	Tonnage	Year	Line	Fate	Deaths
Jul 15, 1928	Cap Lay	8,009	1921	Chargeurs Reunis	typhoon, in Bay of Along	n/a
Nov 12, 1928	Vestris	10,494	1912	Lamport & Holt	cargo shifted, off Hampton Roads	112
Dec 10, 1928	Celtic	20,904	1901	White Star Line	wrecked, at Queenstown	0
Dec 30, 1928	Paul Lecat	12,989	1911	Messageries Maritime	burned, Marseilles	0
Sep 9, 1929	Highland Pride	7,469	1910	Nelson Line	wrecked, off Spain	0
Dec 16, 1929	Manuka	4,534	1903	Union Steamship Co of NZ	wrecked, off New Zealand	0
Dec 18, 1929	Fort Victoria	7,784	1913	Furness, Withy & Co	collision, off New York	0
Jan 22, 1930	Monte Cervantes	13,913	1928	Hamburg-South America Line	wrecked, Straits of Magellan	1
May 21, 1930	Asia	6,122	1907	Fabre Line	burned, at Djibouti	0
May 25, 1930	City of Honolulu	10,860	1900	Los Angeles Steamship Co	burned, at Honolulu	0
Aug 15, 1930	Tahiti	7,585	1904	Union Steamship Co of NZ	engine failure, South Pacific	0
Nov 19, 1930	Highland Hope	14,129	1930	Nelson Line	wrecked, Farilhoes Rocks	1
Apr 2, 1931	Malabar	4,512	1925	Burns, Philip & Co	wrecked, off Sydney	0
Jun 17, 1931	Bermuda	19,086	1927	Furness, Withy & Co	burned, at Hamilton, Bermuda	1
May 16, 1932	Georges Philippar	17,539	1931	Messageries Maritimes	burned, burned off Gulf of Aden	est. 54
Nov 14, 1932	Pieter Corneliszoon Hooft	14,729	1926	Nederland Line	burned, at Amsterdam	0
Jan 4, 1933	L'Atlantique	42,512	1931	Co de Navigation Sud-Atlantique	burned, near English Channel	17
Jun 1, 1933	Guildford Castle	8,001	1911	Union Castle Line	collision, Elbe River	2
Jul 6, 1933	Nicholas Paquet	8,517	1928	Co de Navigation Paquet	wrecked, off North Africa	n/a
Jun 20, 1934	Dresden	14,690	1915	North German Lloyd	wrecked, off Norway	est. 4
Sep 8, 1934	Morro Castle	11,520	1930	Ward Line	burned, off New Jersey	137
Dec 19, 1934	Orania	9,763	1922	Royal Holland Lloyd	collision, at Leixoes	0
Sep 5, 1935	Doric	16,484	1923	White Star Line	collision, off Cape Finisterre	0
Oct 18, 1935	Ausonia	12,955	1928	Soc Italiana di Servizi Maritimi	burned, at Alexandria	3

Date	Ship	Tonnage	Year	Line	Cause/Location	Deaths
Aug 14, 1936	Eubee	9,645	1922	Chargeurs Reunis	collision, near Rio Grande	n/a
Oct 24, 1936	Cristobol Colon	10,833	1923	Co Transatlantica Espanola	wrecked, off Bermuda	0
Dec 10, 1937	President Hoover	21,936	1931	Dollar Line	wrecked, off Formosa	0
Jan 2, 1938	Guaruja	4,282	1921	Co de Nav France-Amerique	wrecked, near Punta Polacra	n/a
May 4, 1938	Lafayette	25,178	1930	Cie Generale Transatlantique	burned, at Le Havre	0
Aug 7, 1938	Reliance	19,618	1915	Hamburg American Line	burned, at Hamburg	0
Apr 19, 1939	Paris	34,569	1921	Cie Generale Transatlantique	burned, at Le Havre	0
Sep 3, 1939	Athenia	13,465	1923	Anchor-Donaldson Line	torpedoed, off Ireland	112
Nov 26, 1939	Pegu	8,016	1921	Burmah Steamship Co	wrecked, near Liverpool	0
Dec 29, 1939	Cabo San Antonio	12,275	1930	Ybarra y Cia	burned, South Atlantic	5
Jan, 1940	President Quezon	14,187	1920	Philippine Mail Line	wrecked, at Riukiu Islands	n/a
Jun 19, 1940	Niagara	13,415	1913	Canadian-Austraasian Line	mined, in Hauraki Gulf	0
Apr 25, 1949	Magdalena	17,547	1949	Royal Mail Line	wrecked, off Rio de Janeiro	0
Nov 4, 1951	Maipu	11,515	1951	Cia Argentina de Nav Dodero	wrecked, near Weser Lightship	0
Dec 22, 1952	Champollion	12,546	1925	Messageries Maritimes	wrecked, off Beirut	15
Jan 8, 1953	Klipfontein	10,544	1939	United Netherlands Nav Co	wrecked, off Cape Barra	0
Jan 25, 1953	Empress of Canada (ex-Duchess of Richmond)	20,325	1928	Canadian Pacific	Burned, Gladstone Drydock	0
Apr 15, 1956	Altair	6,410	1950	Rotterdam South America Line	wrecked, near Vitoria, Brazil	n/a
Jul 25, 1956	Andrea Doria	29,083	1953	Italian Line	collision, off Nantucket	51
Sep 25, 1957	Hildebrand	7,735	1951	Booth Line	wrecked, near Lisbon	0

Date	Ship	Tonnage	Year	Line	Fate	Lost
Nov 2, 1957	Neptunia	10,519	1920	Greek Line	wrecked, off Cobh	0
Mar 31, 1958	Skubryn	9,786	1951	I. M. Skaugen	burned, Indian Ocean	0
Jan 30, 1959	Hans Hedtoft	2,875	1958	Royal Greenland Trading Co	collision, off Greenland	95
Oct 22, 1960	Alcoa Corsair	8,481	1947	Alcoa Steamship Co	collision, in Mississippi	10
Dec 14, 1960	Tarsus	9,451	1931	Turkish Maritime Lines	burned, in Bosphorus	0
Apr 7, 1961	Dara	5,030	1948	British India Steam Nav Co	burned, at Dubai	238
Jul 8, 1961	Save	2,037	1951	Companhia Colonial de Navegacao	burned, off Mozambique	259
Oct 22, 1961	Bianca C	18,427	1944	Costa Armatori	burned, at Granada	4
Mar 14, 1962	Venezuala (ex-De Grasse, ex-Empress of Australia)	18,769	1924	Sicuia Oceanica Societa per Azioni	wrecked, off Cannes	0
Apr 8, 1963	Brittany	16,644	1952	Chandris Lines	burned, at Greece	0
Dec 22, 1963	Lakonia (ex-Johan van Oldenbarnevelt)	20,314	1930	Greek Line	burned, off Canary Islands	89
Nov 19, 1964	Rio de la Plata	11,317	1950	Flota Mercante del Estado	burned, at Buenos Aires	0
Nov 13, 1965	Yarmouth Castle (ex-Evangeline)	5,002	1927	Yarmouth Cruise Lines	burned, off Bahamas	87
Apr 8, 1966	Viking Princess (ex-Lavoisier)	12,812	1950	A/S Berge Sigval Bergesen	burned, off Guantanamo Bay	0
Sep 7, 1966	Hanseatic (ex-Empress of Japan, ex-Empres of Scotland)	30,030	1930	Hamburg-Atlantic Line	burned, at Port Everglades	0
Dec 12, 1966	Heraklion (ex-Leicestershire)	8,922	1949	Typaldos Lines	sunk, off Greece	241

Date	Ship	Tonnage	Year	Line	Fate	Deaths
Mar 20, 1968	Elisabethville	10,901	1948	Compagnie Maritime Belge	burned, at Antwerp	0
Apr 11, 1968	Wahine	8,948	1966	Union Steamship Co of NZ	wrecked, off Wellington	51
Apr 17, 1968	Rio Jachal	11,342	1950	Flota Mercante del Estado	burned, Buenos Aires	0
May 21, 1968	Blenheim	4,766	1951	Fred Olsen & Co	burned, North Sea	0
Jan 24, 1969	Fairsea	13,317	1942	Alvion Steamship Corp	burned, off Balboa	0
Mar 5, 1969	Caribia (ex-Caronia)	34,274	1948	Universal Line	wrecked, at Guam	0
Aug 12, 1969	Paraguay Star	10,722	1948	Blue Star Line	burned, at London	0
Jul 20, 1970	Fulvia	16,923	1949	Costa Armatoria	burned, off Canary Islands	0
Jan 8, 1971	Antilles	19,828	1953	Cie Generale Transatlantique	burned, off Mustique	0
Aug 28, 1971	Helcanna	11,674	1954	C. S. Efthymiadis Line	burned, near Brindisi	24
Sep 8, 1971	Monte Udala	10,170	1948	Naviera Aznar	sank, off Ilheus	0
Jan 9, 1972	Seawise University (ex-Queen Elizabeth)	83,673	1940	C. Y. Tung	burned, at Hong Kong	0
Mar 5, 1972	Marmara	6,042	1956	Turkish Maritime Lines	burned, at the Gold Horn	0
May 25, 1972	Oriental Warrior (ex-Hamburg)	8,269	1954	United Overseas Export Line	burned, off Daytona Beach	0
Sep 23, 1972	Caribia (ex-Vulcania)	24,496	1928	Sicula Oceanica Societa per Azioni	wrecked, at Cannes	0
May 3, 1973	Knossos	10,886	1953	C. S. Efthymiadis Line	burned, off Greece	0
Jun 30, 1973	Satrustegui	6,615	1948	Co Transatlantica Espanola	burned, at Barcelona	0
Jul 1, 1973	Homeric (ex-Mariposa)	18,563	1931	Home Lines	burned, off New York	0
May 12, 1974	Malaysia Kita	11,792	1952	Fir Line	burned, at Singapore	0
Sep 12, 1974	Cunard Ambassador	14,160	1972	Cunard Line	burned, off Key West	0
Jul 30, 1976	Belle Abeto (ex-Laennec)	12,177	1951	Compania de Navigation Abeto	burned, at Sasebo	0
Aug 23, 1976	Malaysia Raya (ex-Laos)	11,792	1954	Fir Line	burned, at Port Kelang	0
Nov 12, 1976	Blue Sea (ex-Europa)	11,340	1952	Ahmed Mohammed Baahoud	burned, at Jeddah	0
Dec 18, 1976	Mecca (ex-Gullfoss)	3,858	1950	Orri Navigation Lines	burned, at Jeddah	0
Dec 25, 1976	Patra (ex-Kronprins Frederik)	3,920	1941	Arab Navigators	burned, off Saudi Arabia	est. 100

Date	Ship	Tonnage	Year	Company	Fate	Deaths
Jun 2, 1977	Rasa Sayang (ex Bergensfjord)	18,739	1956	Michaelis Strouhakis	burned, in Strait of Malacca	2
Mar 30, 1979	Angelina (ex-Oranje)	24,377	1939	Achille Lauro	burned, at St. Thomas	0
Mar 3, 1980	Leonardo Da Vinci	33,340	1960	Italian Line	burned, at La Spezia	0
Apr 24, 1980	Ernesto Anastasio	7,295	1955	Compania Transmediterranea	wrecked, off Spain	0
Aug 27, 1980	Rasa Sayang (ex Bergensfjord)	18,739	1956	CTC Lines	burned, at Perama	0
Oct 4, 1980	Prinsendam	8,566	1973	Holland America Cruises	burned, Gulf of Alaska	0
May 28, 1981	Reina Del Mar (ex-Ocean Monarch)	13,581	1951	Dolphin (Hellas) Shipping	burned, at Perama	0
Aug 20, 1981	Syria	4,423	1962	Egyptian Navigation Co	wrecked, off Crete	0
Dec 20, 1981	Arion	6,400	1965	Maritime Co of Lesvos	burned, at Haifa	0
Aug 8, 1982	Mediterranean Star (ex-Bloemfontein Castle)	16,259	1950	Karageogris Lines	burned, in the Aegean	0
Oct 19, 1982	Ciudad de Sevilla (ex-Infanta Beatrix)	6,368	1927	Compaia Transmediterranea	wrecked, at Majorca	0
Mar 7, 1983	Atlantis (ex-Adonis)	4,505	1965	K-Hellenic Lines	burned, at Piraeus	0
Jul 29, 1984	Columbus C (ex-Kungsholm)	16,317	1953	Costa Armatori	wrecked, at Cadiz	0
Feb 12, 1985	Chidambaram (ex-Pasteur)	17,226	1966	Shipping Corp of India	burned, off Madras	40
Feb 16, 1986	Mikhail Lermontov	20,027	1972	Baltic Shipping Co	wrecked, off New Zealand	1
Aug 31, 1986	Admiral Nakhimov (ex-Berlin)	17,053	1925	Black Sea Shipping Co	collision, in the Black Sea	398

Nearer, my God, to Thee,
　　Nearer to Thee;
E'en though it be a cross
　　That raiseth me;
Still all my song shall be,
"Nearer, my God, to Thee,
　　Nearer to Thee."

Appendix II

WORST PASSENGER LINER LOSSES OF LIFE SINCE 1900

The shipwrecks contained in this section are limited to those passenger liners that were wrecked in peacetime or in wartime while engaged in scheduled passenger service. Only those disasters resulting in one hundred or more deaths have been listed.

DATE	SHIP	TONS	BUILT	COMPANY	NATURE OF DISASTER	LOSS
Apr 14, 1912	Titanic	46,238	1912	White Star Line	collision, in North Atlantic	1,503
May 1, 1915	Lusitania	31,550	1907	Cunard Line	torpedoed, off Ireland	1,198
May 29, 1914	Empress of Ireland	14,191	1905	Canadian Pacific	collision, in St. Lawrence	1,012
Apr, 1902	Camorta	2,119	1880	British India Steam Nav Co	storm, Gulf of Martaban	739
Jan 20, 1920	Afrique	5,404	1907	Chargeur Reunis	wrecked, off Bay of Biscay	553
Jun 28, 1904	Norge	3,310	1881	Scandanavian American Line	wrecked, off Rockall	est. 550
Sep 12, 1919	Valbanera	5,099	1906	Pinillos, Izquierdo y Compania	storm, off Cuba	488
Aug 4, 1906	Sirio	4,141	1883	Raggio Line	wrecked, off Hormigas Island	442
Mar 3, 1916	Principe de Austurias	8,371	1914	Pinillos, Izquierdo y Compania	wrecked, off Brazil	415
Aug 31, 1986	Admiral Nakhimov (ex-Berlin)	17,053	1925	Black Sea Shipping Co	collision, in the Black Sea	398
Oct 25, 1927	Principessa Mafalda	9,210	1909	Nav Gen Italiana Societa	explosion, off Brazil	303
Jul 8, 1961	Save	2,037	1951	Companhia Colonial de Navegacao	burned, off Mozambique	259
Apr 7, 1961	Dara	5,030	1948	British India Steam Nav Co	burned, at Dubai	238
Dec 12, 1966	Heraklion (ex-Leicestershire)	8,922	1949	Typaldos Lines	sunk, off Greece	241
Nov 8, 1915	Ancona	8,885	1908	Italia Line	torpedoed, North Atlantic	194
Sep 8, 1934	Morro Castle	11,520	1930	Ward Line	burned, off New Jersey	137
Oct 9, 1913	Volturno	3,581	1906	Uranium Steamship Co	burned, North Atlantic	136
Nov 12, 1928	Vestris	10,494	1912	Lamport & Holt	cargo shifted, off Hampton Roads	112
Sep 3, 1939	Athenia	13,465	1923	Anchor-Donaldson Line	torpedoed, off Ireland	112
Feb 22, 1901	City of Rio de Janeiro	3,548	1878	Pacific Mail Steamship Co	wrecked, off San Francisco	105
Nov 14, 1909	La Seyne	2,379	1873	Messageries Maritimes	collision, in Rheo Straits	101
Dec 25, 1976	Patra (ex-Kronprins Frederik)	3,920	1941	Arab Navigators	burned, off Saudi Arabia	est. 100

Nearer, My God, to Thee.

There let my way appear,
            Steps unto heaven,
All that Thou sendest me
            In mercy given,
Angels to beckon me,
Nearer, my God, to Thee,
            Nearer to Thee.

Appendix III

LARGEST PASSENGER LINERS LOST SINCE 1900

The shipwrecks contained in this section are limited to those passenger liners that were wrecked in peacetime or in wartime while engaged in scheduled passenger service. Only those ships measuring 20,000 tons or more have been listed.

DATE	SHIP	TONS	BUILT	COMPANY	NATURE OF DISASTER	LOSS
Jan 9, 1972	Seawise University (ex-Queen Elizabeth)	83,673	1940	C. Y. Tung	burned, at Hong Kong	0
Apr 14, 1912	Titanic	46,238	1912	White Star Line	collision, in North Atlantic	1,503
Jan 4, 1933	L'Atlantique	42,512	1931	Co de Navigation Sud Atlantique	burned, near English Channel	17
Apr 19, 1939	Paris	34,569	1921	Cie Generale Transatlantique	burned, at Le Havre	0
Mar 5, 1969	Caribia (ex-Caronia)	34,274	1948	Universal Line	wrecked, at Guam	0
Mar 3, 1980	Leonardo Da Vinci	33,340	1960	Italian Line	burned, at La Spezia	0
May 1, 1915	Lusitania	31,550	1907	Cunard Line	torpedoed, off Ireland	1,198
Sep 7, 1966	Hanseatic (ex-Empress of Japan, ex-Empres of Scotland)	30,030	1930	Hamburg-Atlantic Line	burned, at Port Everglades	0
Jul 25, 1956	Andrea Doria	29,083	1953	Italian Line	collision, off Nantucket	51
May 4, 1938	Lafayette	25,178	1930	Cie Generale Transatlantique	burned, at Le Havre	0
Sep 23, 1972	Caribia (ex-Vulcania)	24,496	1928	Sicula Oceanica Societa per Azioni	wrecked, at Cannes	0
Mar 30, 1979	Angelina (ex-Oranje)	24,377	1939	Achille Lauro	burned, at St. Thomas	0
Dec 10, 1937	President Hoover	21,936	1931	Dollar Line	wrecked, off Formosa	0
Dec 10, 1928	Celtic	20,904	1901	White Star Line	wrecked, at Queenstown	0
Mar 7, 1907	Dakota	20,714	1905	Great Northern Steam Ship Co	wrecked, near Yokohama	0
Jan 25, 1953	Empress of Canada (ex-Duchess of Richmond)	20,325	1928	Canadian Pacific	Burned, Gladstone Drydock	0
Dec 22, 1963	Lakonia (ex-Johan van Oldenbarnevelt)	20,314	1930	Greek Line	burned, off Canary Islands	89
Feb 16, 1986	Mikhail Lermontov	20,027	1972	Baltic Shipping Co	wrecked, off New Zealand	1

"Save, Lord, we perish," was their cry,
"O save us in our agony!"
Thy word above the storm rose high
"Peace, be still."

DEDICATION

This book is dedicated to the memory of Robert T. Mason, a steamship enthusiast of the first rank.
He was a true friend and is sorely missed by all who knew him.

ACKNOWLEDGEMENTS

As I stated in my first steamship book, published only last year, no book is the work of one man.
There are, inevitably, many contributors, both direct and indirect. Some are consciously supportive,
while others contribute in valuable ways without even being aware of the contribution they are
making. My mother falls into the latter category, for it was she who got me started on this whole
affair thirty years ago with a gift of a copy of Walter Lord's celebrated *Titanic* book, *A Night to
Remember*. There are others who have made a more direct effort, such as Richard Faber, one of the
principal dealers in steamship memorabilia in this country, and James R. Moody, who spent many
hours making slides of some of the rarer items reproduced herein so that the originals would not have
to be sent off to an uncertain fate. Laura Brown, librarian of the Steamship Historical Society
Collection at the University of Baltimore, was likewise of inestimable assistance. Several published
works were useful in my research. These included Arnold Kludas' massive six volume set, *Great
Passenger Ships of the World*, Milton Watson's excellent, *Disasters at Sea*, A.A. Hoehling's, *Great
Ship Disasters*, and Roy Anderson's marvelous and, alas, out-of-print, *White Star*. They have all
been instrumental in creating whatever value is contained within these pages and, to all, my thanks.

PUBLISHED BY THOMAS E. BONSALL AND EDWARD A. LEHWALD
THROUGH BOOKMAN PUBLISHING

WRITTEN AND EDITED BY THOMAS E. BONSALL

GRAPHIC DESIGN BY THOMAS E. BONSALL AND JUDY CRAVEN-MADISON

GRAPHIC PRODUCTION BY HAHN GRAPHICS